READER'S DIGEST

THE MIGHTY
OCEANS

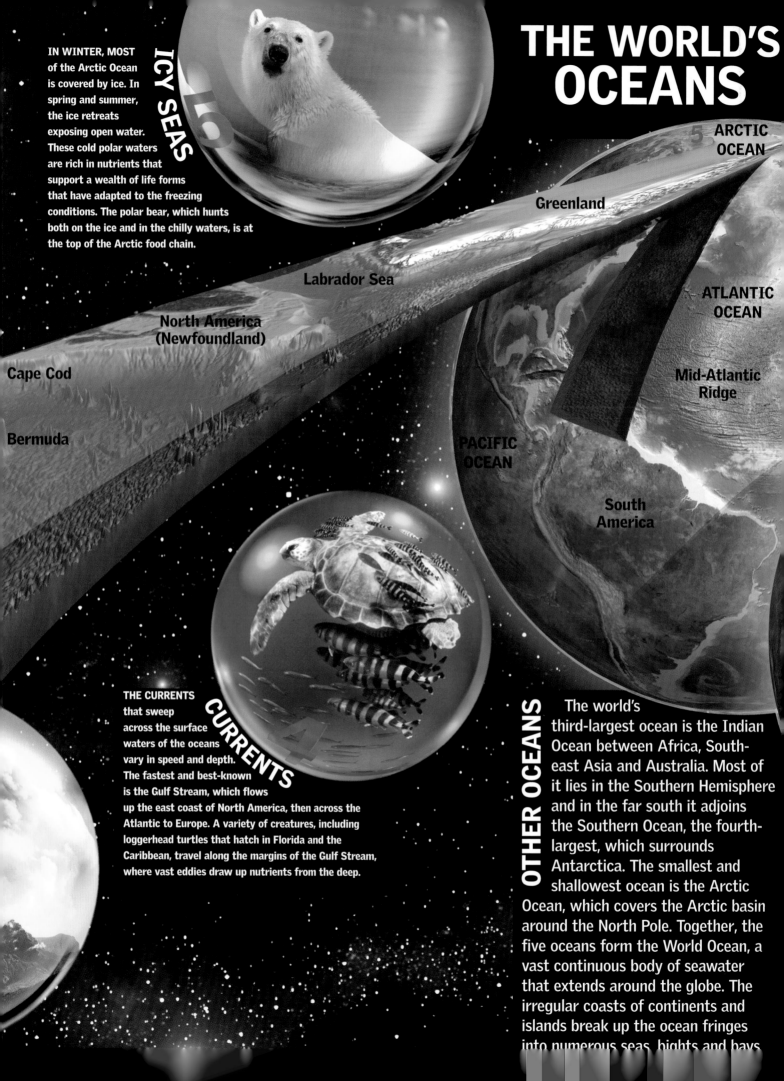

THE WORLD'S OCEANS

ARCTIC OCEAN

ICY SEAS

IN WINTER, MOST of the Arctic Ocean is covered by ice. In spring and summer, the ice retreats exposing open water. These cold polar waters are rich in nutrients that support a wealth of life forms that have adapted to the freezing conditions. The polar bear, which hunts both on the ice and in the chilly waters, is at the top of the Arctic food chain.

Greenland

Labrador Sea

North America (Newfoundland)

Cape Cod

Bermuda

ATLANTIC OCEAN

Mid-Atlantic Ridge

PACIFIC OCEAN

South America

CURRENTS

THE CURRENTS that sweep across the surface waters of the oceans vary in speed and depth. The fastest and best-known is the Gulf Stream, which flows up the east coast of North America, then across the Atlantic to Europe. A variety of creatures, including loggerhead turtles that hatch in Florida and the Caribbean, travel along the margins of the Gulf Stream, where vast eddies draw up nutrients from the deep.

OTHER OCEANS

The world's third-largest ocean is the Indian Ocean between Africa, Southeast Asia and Australia. Most of it lies in the Southern Hemisphere and in the far south it adjoins the Southern Ocean, the fourth-largest, which surrounds Antarctica. The smallest and shallowest ocean is the Arctic Ocean, which covers the Arctic basin around the North Pole. Together, the five oceans form the World Ocean, a vast continuous body of seawater that extends around the globe. The irregular coasts of continents and islands break up the ocean fringes into numerous seas, bights and bays

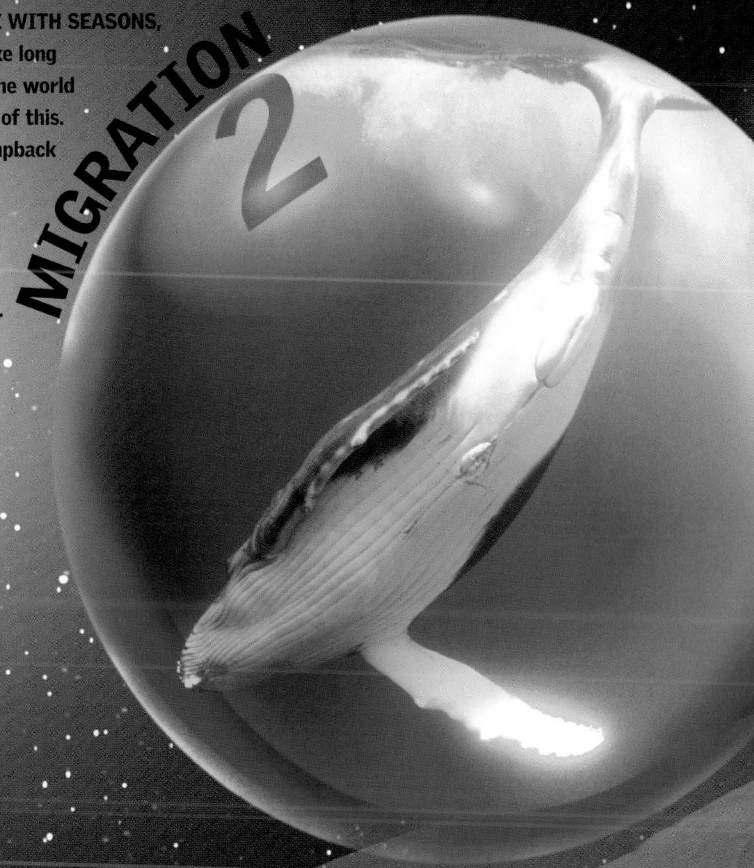

OCEAN CONDITIONS CHANGE WITH SEASONS, and many ocean-dwellers make long migrations from one part of the world to another to take advantage of this. Each spring, for instance, humpback whales travel from breeding grounds off the coast of the Dominican Republic to rich feeding waters in the Gulf of Maine, just north of Cape Cod. When summer ends, they return to warmer waters where they mate and give birth to their young.

MIGRATION 2

THE ATLANTIC

The second-largest of the oceans, the Atlantic separates Europe and Africa from the Americas. It has two large ocean basins, the North and South Atlantic, and an average depth of 3660m. A submarine mountain range, the Mid-Atlantic Ridge, stretches from Iceland almost to Antarctica. The Ridge marks a fault line where plates in the Earth's crust are moving apart. As a result, the Atlantic is growing wider, at about the same rate as human fingernails grow. For its size, it has relatively few islands. The majority are in the Caribbean; most others are either extensions of the continents, such as the UK, or exposed peaks, such as the Azores and Ascension along the Mid-Atlantic Ridge.

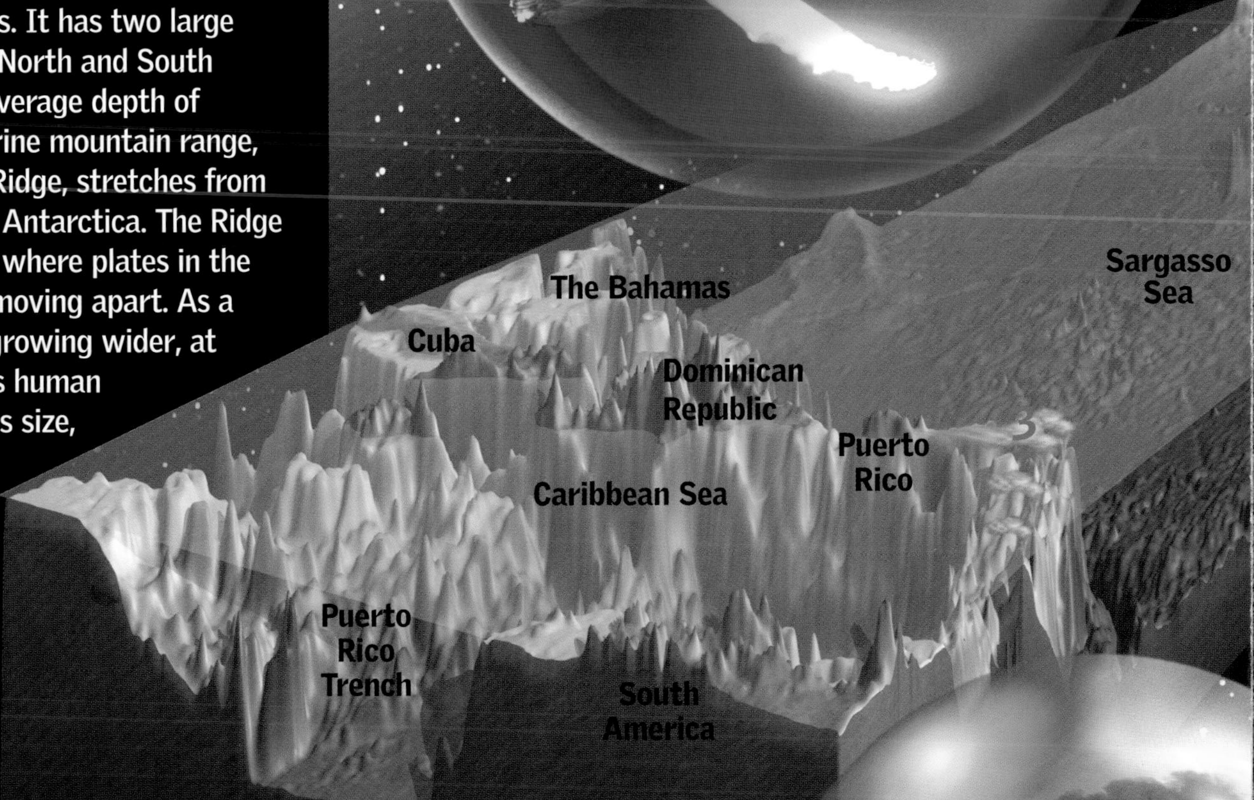

The Bahamas

Cuba

Dominican Republic

Puerto Rico

Caribbean Sea

Sargasso Sea

Puerto Rico Trench

South America

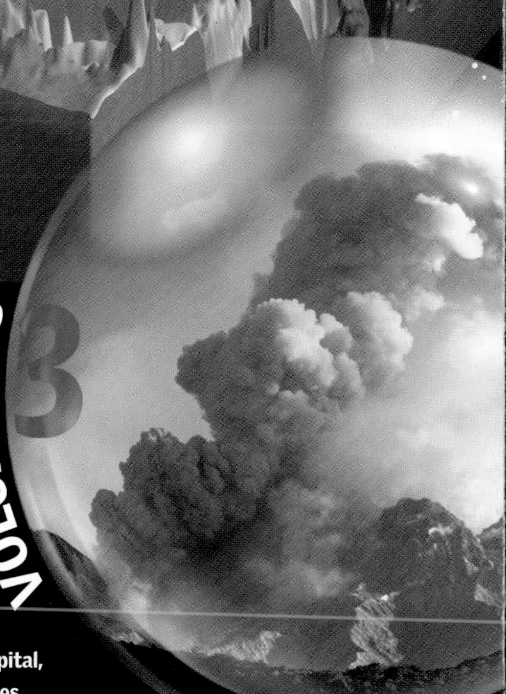

THE MID-ATLANTIC RIDGE is not the only plate boundary beneath the Atlantic. In the west, the North American Plate meets the smaller Caribbean Plate, and the boundary is marked by regular volcanic activity. Many Caribbean islands were born this way, and just as they were created, so they can be destroyed. Between 1995 and 1997, a series of eruptions left much of Montserrat uninhabitable, with pyroclastic flows completely burying the capital, Plymouth. Other islands with active volcanoes include Guadeloupe, Saint Vincent and Martinique.

VOLCANOES 3

OCEANS DOMINATE OUR CLIMATE AND WEATHER EVEN THOUSANDS OF LIFE BEGAN IN OCEAN THE WORLD'S MOST HABITAT, HOME TO AN OF LIFE. YET THEY ARE MOST MYSTERIOUS THE EARTH'S

PLANET. THEY INFLUENCE ALL OVER THE WORLD, MILES FROM THE SEA. WATERS AND THEY ARE DYNAMIC NATURAL AMAZING DIVERSITY THE LEAST EXPLORED, ENVIRONMENT OF ALL – FINAL FRONTIER.

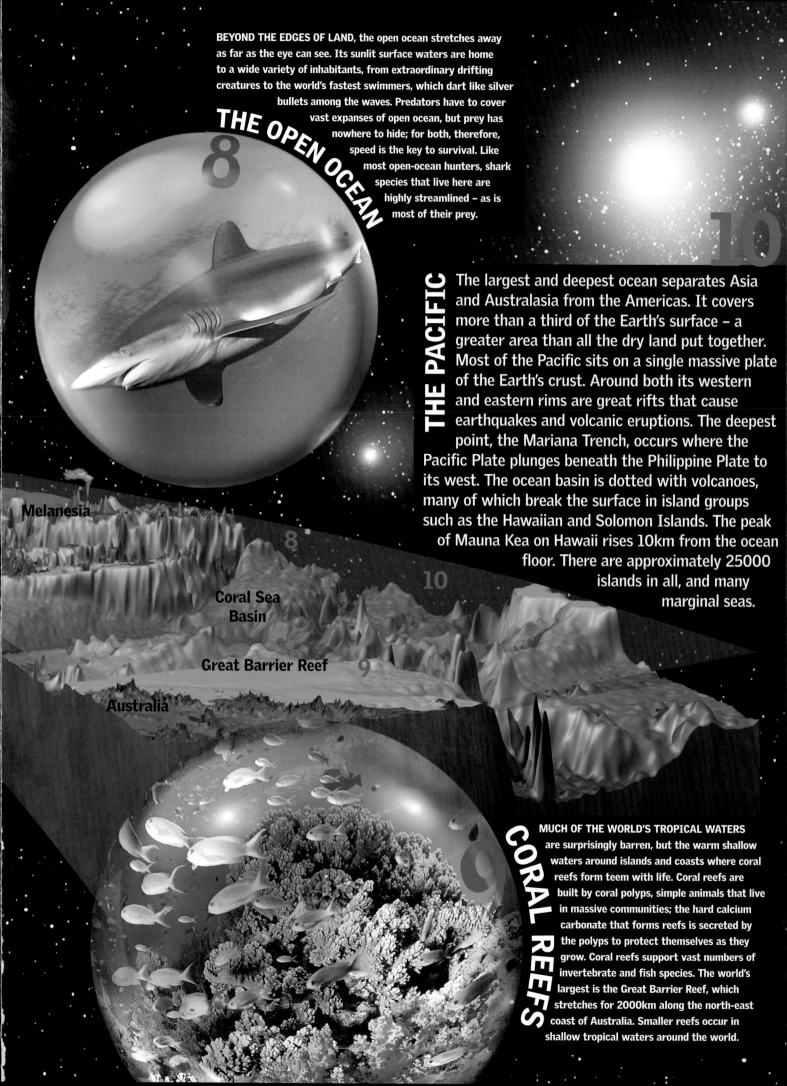

THE OPEN OCEAN

BEYOND THE EDGES OF LAND, the open ocean stretches away as far as the eye can see. Its sunlit surface waters are home to a wide variety of inhabitants, from extraordinary drifting creatures to the world's fastest swimmers, which dart like silver bullets among the waves. Predators have to cover vast expanses of open ocean, but prey has nowhere to hide; for both, therefore, speed is the key to survival. Like most open-ocean hunters, shark species that live here are highly streamlined – as is most of their prey.

THE PACIFIC

The largest and deepest ocean separates Asia and Australasia from the Americas. It covers more than a third of the Earth's surface – a greater area than all the dry land put together. Most of the Pacific sits on a single massive plate of the Earth's crust. Around both its western and eastern rims are great rifts that cause earthquakes and volcanic eruptions. The deepest point, the Mariana Trench, occurs where the Pacific Plate plunges beneath the Philippine Plate to its west. The ocean basin is dotted with volcanoes, many of which break the surface in island groups such as the Hawaiian and Solomon Islands. The peak of Mauna Kea on Hawaii rises 10km from the ocean floor. There are approximately 25000 islands in all, and many marginal seas.

Melanesia

Coral Sea Basin

Great Barrier Reef

Australia

CORAL REEFS

MUCH OF THE WORLD'S TROPICAL WATERS are surprisingly barren, but the warm shallow waters around islands and coasts where coral reefs form teem with life. Coral reefs are built by coral polyps, simple animals that live in massive communities; the hard calcium carbonate that forms reefs is secreted by the polyps to protect themselves as they grow. Coral reefs support vast numbers of invertebrate and fish species. The world's largest is the Great Barrier Reef, which stretches for 2000km along the north-east coast of Australia. Smaller reefs occur in shallow tropical waters around the world.

OCEAN DEPTHS

THE DEEP SEA is by far the largest natural habitat on Earth, including as it does the majority of the water in the oceans. This dark, cold world hides many mysteries, and bizarre new creatures are continually being discovered. Deprived of light, most inhabitants of the deep rely for their food on a 'marine snow' of dead matter that drifts down from above; some creatures produce their own light. Life survives even in the deepest pits of the seabed. This amphipod crustacean, a relative of the woodlouse, can be found in the Mariana Trench, the deepest place on Earth.

HEAVENLY BODIES

THE GREAT MASS OF WATER in the oceans is influenced by forces from beyond our own planet, and this in turn affects conditions on Earth. The twice daily rise and fall of the tides is a direct result of the gravitational force of the Moon, increased or modified by the position of the Sun. When the Moon and the Sun are on opposite sides of the Earth, the Sun's gravitational force cancels out some of the Moon's, causing the lowest tides – called neap tides. When the Sun and Moon are directly in line on the same side of the Earth, their gravitational forces combine to create the highest – spring – tides.

Sea of Japan

China

East China Sea

South China Sea

Philippine Sea

Mariana Trench

Caroline Islands

New Guinea

PACIFIC OCEAN

INDIAN OCEAN

Australia

SOUTHERN OCEAN

FASCINATING FACT

South of Tasmania, in water 1-2km deep, is a field of 70 extinct volcanoes, or seamounts. An array of creatures feed in the forests of coral and sponges near the tops of these underwater islands, and on the food that collects on their isolated slopes. Many are unique, having evolved to live in strong currents in deep waters, among them a squid that emits luminous ink and a giant sea spider.

PERPETUAL MOTION

WAVES ARE DRIVEN by the wind and can travel immense distances across the surface of the open ocean. When they reach shallow coastal water, they bunch up and increase in height before breaking on the shore. The biggest true waves are caused by storms out at sea and are amplified by topographical features on the seabed near the shore. Tsunamis – sometimes, incorrectly, called tidal waves – are not true waves, but the result of submarine earthquakes or other cataclysmic phenomena.

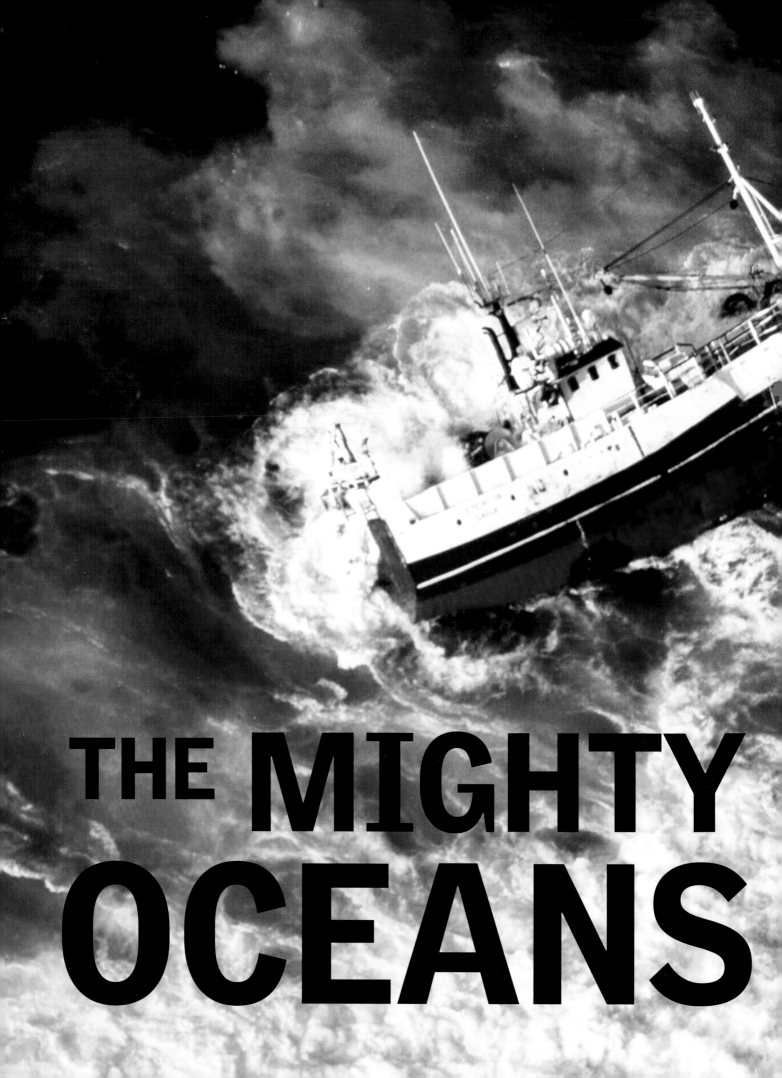

THE MIGHTY OCEANS

1 THE BLUE PLANET

2 MIGHTY CURRENTS

5 GIANTS

6 LIFE IN THE OPEN OCEAN

INTRODUCTION

WE LIVE IN A WORLD DOMINATED BY WATER. IT IS THE MOST COMMON SUBSTANCE ON THE SURFACE OF THE PLANET, AND VIRTUALLY ALL OF IT IS IN THE OCEANS. The influence of all this water is far-reaching: the oceans affect the climate and weather in all regions of the world, even in the centres of vast continents. It was the oceans that once provided a fruitful environment for life to develop on Earth, and they still support the greatest variety of living things, from microscopic algae to the largest creature on the planet today, the blue whale.

This book explores the many realms that exist in the world's oceans and the enormous **variety of life** that inhabits them – from the **sunlit surface** to the **darkest depths**; from the vastness of the **open oceans** to the **reefs and coasts** around their margins; from the icy seas of the **polar regions** to the Sun-warmed waters of **the tropics**. It reveals secrets only recently discovered, as the latest technology and exploration techniques bring **inaccessible areas** within reach. Above all, it offers insight into this most extensive and powerful of Earth's natural domains, into the mighty forces that created it and that drive its restless cycles, and the violence it can unleash upon the land.

The oceans are **Earth's most dynamic environment**. They contain about 1.35 billion km³ of water, and this huge mass is constantly on the move. The surface waters rock back and forth as **waves** pass over, from gentle ripples to powerful swells whipped up by storms. Twice a day, in response to the gravitational forces of the Sun and Moon, the **tides** rise and fall, their continual motion gradually eroding and shaping the land.

The surfaces of the oceans are dominated by **wind-driven currents**, which can carry huge **icebergs** for thousands of miles and spread tropical warmth from the Equator towards the Poles. The **Gulf Stream** that crosses the North Atlantic carries more water than all the world's rivers combined, yet it is but a small part of a much greater system encompassing both surface and deep currents. Winding in an endless loop and connecting the world's oceans together, the system known as the **great ocean conveyor belt** transports oxygen, warmth and nutrients to different parts of the Earth.

Ocean currents also affect **climate and weather** around the world. When currents change, as some do naturally as part of an irregular cycle, the weather changes with them: **El Niño** is a result of changes in the surface currents of the Pacific Ocean that knock the whole world's weather out of kilter. In El Niño years, places that are usually arid become battered by violent storms, while regions normally watered by frequent rains suffer drought and can become tinder dry.

Although the oceans form a continuous body of water, **differences in latitude** create very different conditions. **Polar waters** are frigid but rich in nutrients, and support an astounding **abundance of life**. In winter the Arctic and Southern oceans are shrouded in darkness, but as spring returns and brings the Sun, they become filled with algae and other **plankton**, which provide food for multitudes of **krill and fish**. These in turn support larger fish, marine mammals and birds.

The **waters of the tropics** are much less rich in life. Their azure clarity is due to the relative **lack of plankton** – the root of the ocean food chain. Here, the majority of life is concentrated around **coral reefs**, which generate their own nutrients through a unique partnership between coral polyps and single-celled algae that live in their tissues.

Conditions in the oceans also vary significantly with **changes in depth**. Algal life is concentrated near the surface, where sufficient light penetrates for photosynthesis to occur. In the **deep ocean**, most creatures either hunt others or rely on food that drifts down from above. The deep sea holds many mysteries yet to be uncovered – less than 1 per cent of the seabed has been fully mapped and explored. What is known is that the **ocean floor** is far from the featureless plain once imagined: it is riven by **canyons** and laced with hills, **volcanoes** and towering **mountain ranges**. In places, submarine **geysers** belch out scalding water; in others, lakes of super-dense brine have formed. Yet even in these hostile conditions, life has taken hold.

The shallow **coastal fringes**, where ocean meets land, are much better understood. Here, life faces unique challenges – the rise and fall of tides, the pounding of waves – but it also enjoys many opportunities to thrive as the waters are **nutrient-rich**. Most of the **world's richest fisheries** are in coastal waters, and it is here that most people who make a living from the sea are to be found.

SHALLOW SEAS
An aerial view of the Bahamas, the calm shallow waters between Cuba and Florida, on the western fringe of the Atlantic. The Bahamas are the peaks of a submarine limestone mountain range that built up over 190 million years. It rises 4400 metres above the ocean floor, and breaks the surface in some 700 islands and 2400 reefs. Local people can tell from the colour of the water how far it is to the sandy bottom: at less than 10 metres deep the sea looks turquoise and green; deeper waters appear blue. Seafarers used to call the region the 'baja mar', or shallow sea.

THE B
PLA

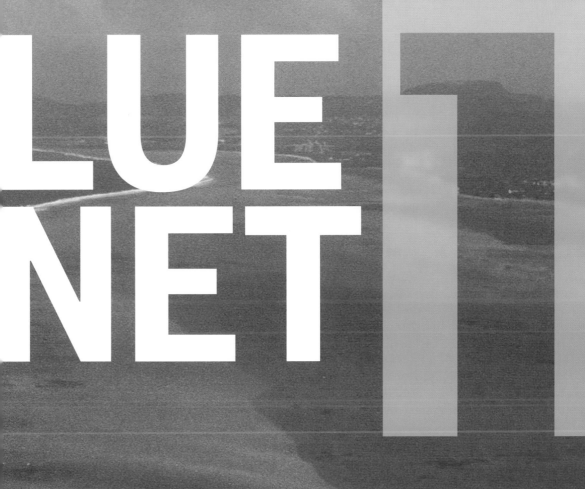

LUE
NET

1

WATER DOMINATES THE SURFACE OF OUR PLANET: MORE THAN TWO-THIRDS OF THE EARTH IS COVERED BY OCEAN, and more than half by waters more than 3 km deep. Not far from this tiny island, perched on top of a coral reef in the western Pacific, the ocean floor plummets into the Mariana Trench, the deepest point on Earth. The ocean depths are the Earth's last true wilderness – a hidden world of submarine mountains, valleys and plains, and the extraordinary creatures that live there. Huge tracts of these depths have yet to be mapped: imagine trying to survey trenches deeper than Mount Everest is tall – and doing it underwater in utter darkness. Even with the most sophisticated technology, some areas may never be explored.

THE WORLD OCEAN

Deep below the surface, submarine currents work like the planet's bloodstream, pumping water between the Equator and the Poles.

HOW MANY OCEANS ARE THERE? Officially, the answer is five, although the fifth – the Southern Ocean – had to wait until the year 2000 to be formally defined. But seawater does not recognise lines that humans draw on maps. Instead, it forms the World Ocean – a huge body of interconnected basins, seas and bays that covers two-thirds of the Earth.

The vastness of this mass of water almost defies imagination. In area, the World Ocean covers more than 300 million km². The USA would fit into it more than 35 times, while there would be enough room for nearly 1500 copies of the British Isles. In three dimensions, rather than just two, the figures become even more staggering. The average depth of the ocean is almost 4 km. In places, the ocean could swallow Mount Everest with 2 km of water to spare. The total volume of water is approximately 1.35 billion km³. This is the equivalent of more than 83 000 Olympic-sized swimming pools of water for every individual currently alive on the Earth.

A world on the move

The waters of this great ocean are constantly in motion, whipped up by the winds, and driven by the rotation of the Earth itself. Ocean water can be slack and sluggish, or it can be thrown into mountainous waves. Where it meets the land it scours beaches and batters headlands, and ebbs and flows through countless creeks and channels as the tides rise and fall. Deep below the surface, submarine currents work like the planet's bloodstream, pumping water between the Equator and the Poles. In some places, ocean water seems to be in a

PACIFIC OCEAN Hundreds of volcanic islands dot the Pacific, many of them inhabited. The East Pacific Rise is a range of underwater mountains, rising up to 3000 m from the seabed.

ATLANTIC OCEAN This is defined as the waters separating the Americas from Europe and Africa. Imaginary lines running from the southernmost tips of South America and Africa divide the Atlantic from the Pacific and Indian Oceans.

hurry, as it surges through narrow straits, or pours over submerged cliffs and sills. Far from the surface, however, in the cold blackness at great depth, it can creep over the seabed at astonishingly sluggish speeds of no more than a few kilometres a year.

As land-dwellers, it is difficult for us to grasp the reality of this seemingly endless fluid space. For midwater fish, the ocean is almost literally infinite – a place filled with strange sounds and living lights, but without any tangible boundaries. For these animals, water is the world. Their only contact with solid objects comes when they eat, or when something eats them. At the surface, the ocean is much more familiar to us, but with its ever-changing moods, and lack of any fixed points, it is still utterly unlike any habitat that exists on dry land.

Early ocean exploration

Because humans live on land, it is only natural that we have used land to try to make sense of this world of water. For the ancient Greeks, the Atlantic was the original 'world ocean': they believed it surrounded the land on Earth and they called it the *pelagos Atlantikos*, the 'sea of Atlas'. The Atlantic is the world's second-largest ocean, after the Pacific, and with its long history of fishing, whaling and scientific investigation, it is the best explored. The Pacific is by far the world's largest ocean, while in third place, the Indian Ocean contains about a fifth of the water in the seas.

In the far north, human hunters have plied the shores of the Arctic Ocean since prehistoric times, but the Southern Ocean, with its violent storms and

icy waters, resisted exploration until the 1770s, when the British navigator James Cook became the first person known to have crossed the Antarctic Circle. With this remarkable and dangerous journey, the true extent of the great World Ocean was finally recognised.

Seas and bays

All of the world's oceans have their own seas and bays, some of which appeared on maps before the oceans themselves had been named. Seas are mostly bounded by coasts, at least in part. The Sea of Japan, for example, is bounded by the coasts of Japan, Russia and the Korean peninsula, while the Mediterranean (from the Latin *mediterraneus*, 'inland'), although technically part of the Atlantic, is almost completely landlocked. Bays are defined more by their coastal borders than by the waters they contain. The world's largest is often said to be Hudson Bay, because of the length of its coastline, but the Bay of Bengal has more water.

CHARTED WATERS OF THE ANCIENTS

The oceans have long provided routes for trade. From ancient times, certain areas bustled with vessels carrying goods between ports. Some of the people who made these journeys took the time to map the coasts and waters they travelled. The people of ancient Egypt, Phoenicia and Crete all made maps of the eastern Mediterranean. The ancient Greeks travelled farther, charting the Strait of Gibraltar and the sea beyond by as early as 900 BC. One of the world's oldest surviving maps, dating from around 2200 BC, was found in Xi'an, the ancient capital of China. Etched on stone and showing incredible detail, it charts the coast of the South China Sea.

INDIAN OCEAN A mid-ocean ridge, surfacing in places as islands, divides the Indian Ocean into eastern and western halves. A line running south from Tasmania separates it from the Pacific.

SOUTHERN OCEAN This surrounds Antarctica, stretching northward to the 60° South line of latitude (marked in red). The International Hydrographic Organization officially set its limits in the spring of 2000.

ARCTIC OCEAN Extending for 14 million km², this is the smallest and shallowest of the oceans, with just 1 per cent of the Earth's saltwater. A thick sheet of ice covers the Arctic for most of the year.

DRIVING THE WEATHER

NO MATTER WHERE YOU LIVE, THE WORLD'S OCEANS AFFECT THE ENVIRONMENT AROUND YOU. The clouds overhead are almost certain to come from ocean water, and the rain that falls from them is likely to have been in the sea just a few days ago. Without clouds, temperature extremes would be much greater, and fresh water would be scarce. Even more significantly, without fresh water, you and all other forms of land-based life would not exist at all.

As well as generating rain and snow through surface evaporation, the oceans act as a heat pump, drawing warm water away from the tropics to bathe coastlines far from the Equator. As a result, some regions are much warmer than they would otherwise be. The British Isles are a prime example: their temperate climate is a direct result of the effects of the Gulf Stream, which flows past their shores. At the same latitude on the opposite side of the Atlantic, a cold current bathes Newfoundland, bringing icebergs drifting past its shores and much colder winters.

Currents affect weather in other ways, too. Where warm and cold currents meet, for example, great banks of fog form. Changes in currents also affect the weather, sometimes on a global scale. Periodically, Pacific Ocean currents that flow off the west coast of South America reverse direction, and this reversal underlies the phenomenon known as El Niño, which has an awesome impact on weather patterns right around the globe.

Storm machine

Oceans do not always transfer heat in a smooth and orderly way. In the tropics, the energy stored up by ocean water can trigger cyclonic storms, which can develop into lethal hurricanes. Fuelled by the oceans' warmth, these storms veer north and south from the tropical zone, creating immense devastation if they hit land.

Hurricanes spawned in the Atlantic regularly cause devastation in the Caribbean Sea and on the eastern and southern seaboards of the USA. The intensity of each storm depends on the temperature of the water offshore. Hurricanes are fuelled by warm surface water, but as they spin, they churn up the water beneath, drawing up more from the depths. If that deeper water is warm, as it is in the Caribbean, it continues to fuel the hurricane. If it is cooler, as in the Gulf of Mexico, the hurricane loses power and can fade away.

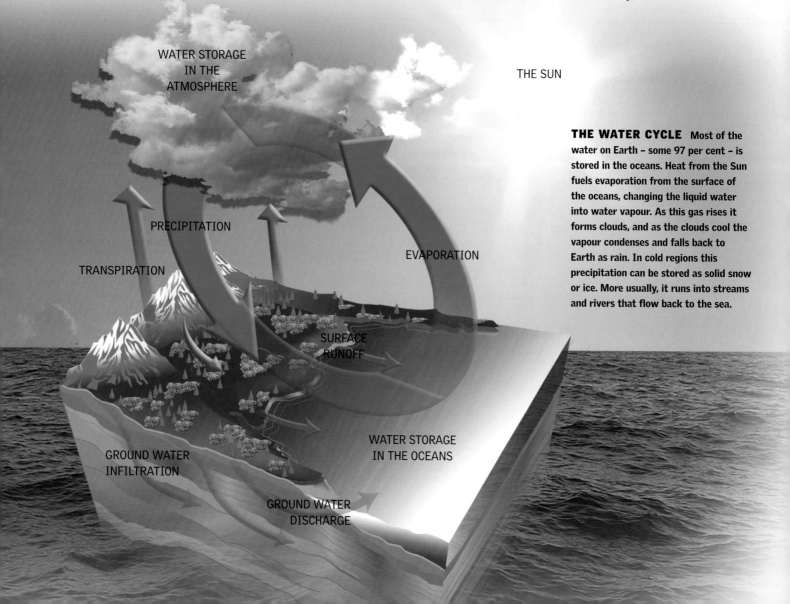

WATER STORAGE IN THE ATMOSPHERE

THE SUN

PRECIPITATION

TRANSPIRATION

EVAPORATION

THE WATER CYCLE Most of the water on Earth – some 97 per cent – is stored in the oceans. Heat from the Sun fuels evaporation from the surface of the oceans, changing the liquid water into water vapour. As this gas rises it forms clouds, and as the clouds cool the vapour condenses and falls back to Earth as rain. In cold regions this precipitation can be stored as solid snow or ice. More usually, it runs into streams and rivers that flow back to the sea.

SURFACE RUNOFF

GROUND WATER INFILTRATION

WATER STORAGE IN THE OCEANS

GROUND WATER DISCHARGE

PACIFIC

THE MIGHTY PACIFIC

THE PACIFIC IS NOT ONLY THE WORLD'S BIGGEST OCEAN BUT ALSO THE DEEPEST. IT COVERS AROUND A THIRD OF THE GLOBE AND CONTAINS MORE THAN HALF OF ALL THE WATER ON THE PLANET. ITS AREA IS GREATER THAN THAT OF ALL THE LAND ON EARTH PUT TOGETHER.

The Pacific is an ocean of superlatives in more than just its overall size. Within its waters are both the deepest point on Earth and, arguably, the highest mountain. The Mariana Trench, near the Mariana Islands, south-east of Japan, bottoms out at 10 920 m. Hawaii's Mauna Kea rises 10 203 m from its base on the seabed to its snow-capped peak – far outstripping Everest's 8850 m from base to peak. The Pacific contains the world's largest living structure, the Great Barrier Reef, which lies off the north-east coast of Australia. The Pacific also has more islands than all the other oceans combined.

The 16th-century Portuguese explorer Ferdinand Magellan gave the ocean its name: he called it the *Mare Pacificum*, meaning 'Peaceful Sea'. While his journey across the Pacific was relatively storm-free, the name was not well-chosen. Much of the Pacific Ocean is prone to hurricanes and typhoons, as well as tsunamis triggered by submarine earthquakes. Its huge size and the remoteness of most of it from the world's large populated land masses has made it one of the least explored places on Earth – it has been said that we know more about the surface of the Moon than what lies in the Pacific's watery depths.

VITAL STATISTICS

AREA: 166 million km^2
COASTLINE: 135 663 km
WIDEST POINT: Strait of Malacca to Colombia, 17 700 km
AVERAGE DEPTH: 4280m
DEEPEST POINT: Mariana Trench 10 920 m

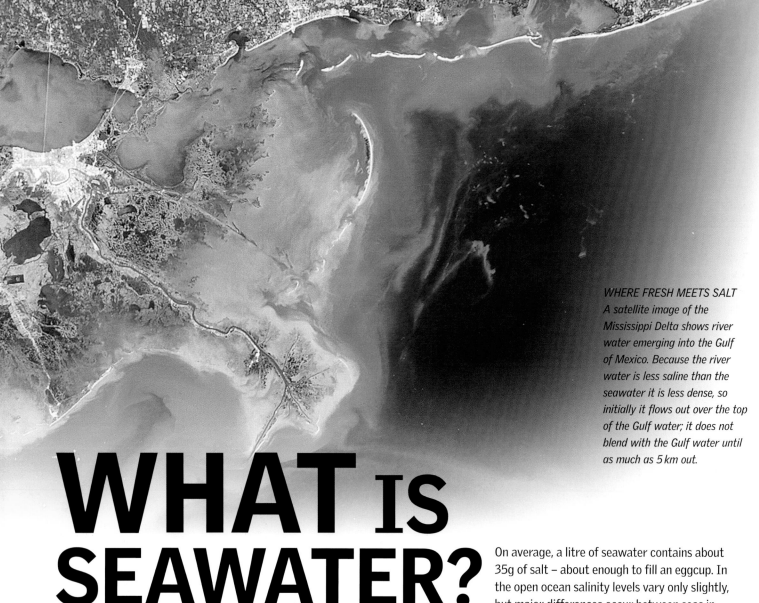

WHAT IS SEAWATER?

SEAWATER IS THE MOST ABUNDANT SUBSTANCE ON THE SURFACE OF THE PLANET. It is also one of the most complex, containing more than 90 different chemical elements – some as common as oxygen, others as rare as gold. In bright sunlight, the clearest seawater looks almost perfectly transparent, with just the slightest hint of blue. In some parts of the world, however, it can appear green, grey or yellow, or as cloudy as milk, because of sediment washed into it from the land.

Ask anyone what is the difference between seawater and fresh water, and they are likely to answer in one word: salt. The salty taste of seawater comes from sodium chloride, as in the common salt that we use on food. Across the world, common salt makes up more than 85 per cent of all the dissolved substances in seawater. If the water was all removed from the oceans and the dissolved substances left behind, sodium chloride would form a layer averaging around 45 m thick. In addition to sodium chloride, seawater contains salts of a number of other elements, including magnesium, calcium and potassium. Many of these salts play an important role in biochemical reactions – a lasting legacy of the fact that life first evolved in the seas.

On average, a litre of seawater contains about 35g of salt – about enough to fill an eggcup. In the open ocean salinity levels vary only slightly, but major differences occur between seas in different world regions. The world's saltiest seawater is wedged between Africa and Arabia, in the northern end of the Red Sea. Here, intense sunshine beats down on practically landlocked water. As a result, it evaporates at record rates, intensifying the salt concentration left behind. At the other extreme, heavy rainfall can dilute the saltiness of surface waters, particularly in places like the Baltic Sea, where the climate is cold and evaporation slow.

These differences in salinity have a marked effect on anything that floats, from seagulls to ocean liners. Extra salt makes seawater more dense, so floating objects are more buoyant. Ships in warm shallow seas can carry heavier cargoes than those travelling on cold deep ones. This is reflected in a ship's Plimsoll line – a gauge painted on the hull to show the maximum safe load for different types of sea.

Why seawater is salty

The oceans originally formed from water vapour, which fell as rain over 4.3 billion years ago. The salt in that seawater came from three separate sources, all of which are still at work today. One is volcanic eruptions. When these occur on the seabed, they inject gases directly into the water. Substances in the gases, such as sulphur and chlorine, react with the water and are transformed as they dissolve. A second source is the weathering of land by rainfall. Rainwater gradually washes salt minerals out of the land, and rivers carry them to the sea.

The third source of salt involves plate tectonics – the process that constantly creates and reshapes the Earth's solid crust. On parts of the seabed, the plates that form the Earth's crust are pulling apart, and the seawater above these gaps reacts with the hot, newly formed rocks below. This process can form salts directly, but seawater is also sucked down into the Earth's crust, to be released later with dissolved salts contained in it. By this very slow but continuous mechanism, all of the ocean's water is circulated every 5-10 million years. It is almost certainly the answer to a conundrum that has for a long time puzzled scientists: why the composition of seawater has been virtually constant for the last 300 million years or so.

FACTS

SEA SALT AND TABLE SALT ARE CHEMICALLY DIFFERENT
Sea salt is 98 per cent sodium chloride but also contains traces of around 90 other minerals. Table salt is 99.9 per cent sodium chloride. The remaining 0.1 per cent is made up of additives, including potassium iodide, aluminium silicate and sugar.

97 **PER CENT** of the world's water is in the seas. The remaining 3 per cent is fresh water, mostly locked in the ice caps.

SEAWATER IS SLIGHTLY
ALKALINE Its normal pH is around 8: that of fresh water is 7.

FACTS

SALT EXTRACTION Salt pans in the state of Tamil Nadu in India. Seawater evaporates in the open 'pans', leaving behind deposits of salt.

OCEAN FOOD CHAIN *Tiny shrimplike creatures called krill are a key element in the Antarctic food chain. Krill feed off algae, and are themselves food for larger creatures from squid to penguins, seals and huge baleen whales.*

Invisible ingredients

Seawater abounds with dissolved gases. Most enter the sea from the atmosphere, although some come from submarine volcanoes or from living things. Not surprisingly, the most common gas in seawater is also the most common in the atmosphere: nitrogen. It makes up about half of all the dissolved gas in the seas.

Carbon dioxide, the second most common gas, is more than 60 times more abundant in the oceans than in air because it is highly soluble in seawater. Much of it is absorbed from the atmosphere at the ocean's surface, but an even larger proportion comes from things living in the sea. Fish and other marine animals release carbon dioxide when they respire, and seabed bacteria release it when they break down dead remains. On the other side of the equation, algae absorb carbon dioxide during photosynthesis – the process by which plants harness energy from sunlight. Because algae live mainly near the surface, there is less carbon dioxide here than at greater depths.

Oxygen for life

Oxygen – vital for animal life in the oceans – is the third most common dissolved gas in seawater. Some comes from algae, which generate oxygen as a waste product of photosynthesis, and this finds its way into the water. Oxygen is four times more abundant than carbon dioxide in the top 40 m of water, where most algae live, but at a depth of around 100 m, the proportions change and carbon dioxide becomes more abundant.

Unlike carbon dioxide, oxygen does not dissolve particularly well in seawater. Most of the oxygen generated by photosynthetic algae leaves the oceans and enters the air. Nevertheless, the flow is two-way, and some atmospheric oxygen does dissolve into seawater. This happens far more easily in cold water than in warm and where wave action agitates the sea's surface, which helps to explain why polar waters often teem with life. Becalmed tropical waters, despite their seductive beauty, are the least productive waters of all.

Diluted seawater

In places such as river estuaries seawater is diluted. Incoming tides meet fresher water flowing in the opposite direction, and the two slowly mix. This mixing is far from even. Because fresh water is lighter than salt water it tends to float to the top; the tidal waters flowing in form a wedge beneath the countercurrent of fresh water above. There is a similar effect around the ice caps, where in spring and summer meltwater dilutes the surrounding seawater. There are fears that global warming will increase the amount of meltwater entering the ocean. If this happens too quickly, a layer of mainly fresh water will start to build up on the sea surface around the Poles, which could affect the world's currents. The Gulf Stream, for example, could be deflected or even shortened, ending before it reaches the coastal waters of Britain and Europe.

Oxygen dissolves into seawater more easily in cold water than in warm, which is one reason why polar waters often teem with life. Despite their seductive beauty, becalmed tropical waters are the least productive of all.

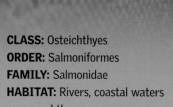

CLASS: Osteichthyes

ORDER: Salmoniformes

FAMILY: Salmonidae

HABITAT: Rivers, coastal waters and the open ocean

KEY FEATURE: They breed in fresh water but spend most of their lives at sea

MANY FISH AND OTHER SEA CREATURES HAVE A FINE SENSE OF SMELL, WHICH THEY USE TO LOCATE FOOD AND OTHER MEMBERS OF THEIR OWN KIND IN THE WATER. Fish smell underwater in much the same way as we do in air, detecting suspended particles with sensory cells in their nostrils. The cells are arranged within the nostril on an organ called the olfactory rosette. The size of the rosette is directly proportional to the ability to smell. Sharks, for example, which have extremely large olfactory rosettes, can smell a potential meal from several hundred metres away.

The ability of fish to smell food has long been known about, but in recent decades scientists have put forward the theory that some species may be able to smell their way around the oceans by detecting subtle differences in the composition of seawater. Although this theory has yet to be proved, one type of fish is known to navigate by smell. Every year adult salmon travel thousands of miles across the ocean to their home rivers, where they spawn. They locate the mouths of these rivers by scent. Every river has its own signature smell, the result of the unique path it takes through the landscape, and the rocks that it flows over on the way. This smell is imprinted on the young salmon when they first travel downriver to the sea – and it stays with them for the rest of their lives. As they near the coast on their return journeys as adults ready to breed, they smell the water, searching for the telltale combination of particles that will lead them to the correct river mouth.

Adult salmon spend most of their time in the sea, but their breeding habits vary. Atlantic salmon spend up to four years in the ocean before returning to breed, gathering in late summer near their home rivers. After swimming upstream and breeding, they return, exhausted, to the sea. By contrast, Pacific sockeye salmon breed only once in their lives. Having travelled upriver, every single adult dies once it has paired up and spawned.

THE DEEP BLUE SEA

SEAWATER HAS NO INTRINSIC COLOUR OF ITS OWN – a glass full of seawater is completely transparent. But when you look out at an expanse of sea on a clear day, it usually looks blue.

A number of factors combine to produce this effect. In part the sea looks blue because its surface is reflecting the blue sky above. But its colour is also the result of the way the sea interacts with sunlight that has penetrated its surface. Some of the light is absorbed, and some of it is scattered or reflected by particles in the water or (in shallower waters) by the seabed.

Sunlight is made up of a mixture of colours from violet and blue through green to yellow, orange and red – the colours of the rainbow. Each colour has its own wavelength and together they make up the visible spectrum; when all the colours of the spectrum are seen simultaneously, they are perceived as white. When sunlight travels through water, some of it is absorbed by water molecules, but the spectrum is not absorbed evenly. Longer wavelengths (corresponding to red, orange and yellow) are absorbed more readily than shorter wavelengths such as the greens and blues. As a result more blue light, and to a lesser extent green, is transmitted through the water. So the sea appears blue or greeny-blue, because the rest of the visible spectrum has been absorbed.

How depth affects colour

The different ways in which water absorbs different wavelengths means that the sea's colour is also affected by the depth of the water. Clear, well-lit and shallow coastal waters, where large amounts of blue and green light reach the sandy seabed and are reflected back, often appear turquoise. Farther out, where the water is deeper, more of the greens are absorbed and the sea

CRYSTAL CLEAR The sparkling waters off Madagascar are typical of warm tropical seas, which contain few nutrients. The waters are rarely cloudy because they have only low levels of plankton and often afford clear views of the bottom. Reflection of green and blue light from the seabed produces the stunning turquoise colour. Farther out, where the water is deeper, it appears blue since more of the green light is being absorbed.

THE OCEAN CAN GLOW AT NIGHT

Blooms of phosphorescent algae sometimes occur in such densities that they illuminate the surface waters of the ocean with an eerie light. Mariners call this phenomenon a 'milky sea'.

THE PACIFIC'S COLOUR can help

scientists to predict an El Niño event. Changes in ocean currents, which cause an El Niño event, also cause blooms of red, green and brown planktonic algae, which can be seen from satellites in space.

Not-so-blue seas

Sometimes, the sea looks grey-green, brown, yellow or even orange or red. Grey-green seas are usually the result of heavily overcast and rainy weather. Heavy clouds filter out much of the red light from sunlight before it even reaches the sea, while rain disturbance of the sea surface interferes with the water's light-transmitting properties. The result is a dark, green-tinged appearance.

Brown seas are generally full of sediment, either churned up from the seabed or dumped in them by rivers. Mud particles act in the opposite way to water molecules, reflecting rather than absorbing red light, so a high concentration of mud particles near the surface will usually turn the sea brown. Mud disgorged by the River Amazon, for example, affects the colour of the Atlantic far offshore, and the Yellow Sea, between China and the Korean peninsula, gets its colour from the fine yellow silt that pours into it from the Yellow River, or Huang He.

Occasionally, living organisms colour the ocean. Every June, huge shoals of pilchards gather off eastern South Africa, turning the water there almost black. Around the continents, particularly Antarctica, an abundance of microscopic organisms with chlorophyll adds to the greenness of the water. When conditions are right, many single-celled species of plankton reproduce rapidly and clog surface waters with large plankton 'blooms', which may turn the ocean pink, orange, brown or purple. A few of these species produce toxins that harm other marine organisms; some colour the water red, hence the concept of harmful 'red tides'.

looks a deeper blue. Very deep water – where the colour is solely the result of reflection or scattering of light by particles in the water – appears very dark blue, sometimes almost black.

The position of the observer also influences the sea's apparent colour. From a beach, the sea is viewed from an acute angle. Shallow water, which might look evenly coloured when seen from above, seems to become darker the farther out it is. This is because light reflected from the seabed farther out has to travel a greater distance through the water before it reaches the beach, so the water that is farther away looks 'deeper', even when it actually is not.

While the surface of the sea may appear turquoise or blue on a calm day, it quickly becomes flecked with white when the weather turns windy. The white water that occurs on the edges of waves, both out to sea and along the shore, is partly caused by seawater breaking up into droplets. The water droplets reflect almost the whole spectrum of visible light and so appear white. Water also appears white where it has formed froth after trapping bubbles of air. The apparent colour is the result of light being reflected by these bubbles.

A healthy colour?

With satellite technology scientists can now monitor the ocean's colour from space. Using instruments that are more sensitive than the human eye, a huge array of colours can be measured that provide information on the amount and type of plankton, sediments and chemicals in any given area. This data relates to the health and chemistry of the ocean and has relevance to environmental issues, such as global warming.

HOW THE OCEANS FORMED

THE OCEANS ARE ALMOST AS OLD AS EARTH ITSELF. Evidence gleaned from the world's oldest surviving rock crystals has shown that our planet had continents, oceans and an atmosphere at least 4.3 billion years ago – just 300 million years after it first formed.

Scientists have two main theories about where the water in the oceans came from. The first of these theories states that it came from Earth itself. When Earth and the other planets originally formed from a cloud of gas and dust surrounding the Sun, some water was present in the cloud. As the material from which Earth was made came together into a sphere, the existing water along with new water formed by chemical reactions was incorporated into the upper layers of the young planet and into its atmosphere. The water trapped as vapour inside the planet's upper layers was soon released into the atmosphere through volcanic eruptions. Then, as the planet cooled, most of the atmospheric water vapour condensed and fell to the surface as rain.

The second theory claims that comets brought the water to Earth. Comets are made partly of water ice, and huge numbers of them crashed into the planet during its early history. As they hit Earth, they would have been obliterated and their contents would have vaporised. Again, the water vapour they released would have condensed and fallen as rain.

These theories are not mutually exclusive. Rather, scientists divide into two camps over which of the processes was the more important source of Earth's ocean water. Most agree that both probably played some role: in other words, some of the water was home-grown and some of it extra-terrestrial.

The origin of ocean basins

By the time water first started raining down on Earth, there was probably already some higher ground – the rudimentary continents – on its surface, interspersed with depressions which the water filled. The process by which these raised landmasses and depressions appeared is believed to have started within a few hundred million years of Earth's formation, when the planet had cooled sufficiently for a solid crust to form at its surface, floating on a layer of magma (liquid rock). The crust soon broke up into a number of large chunks, which shifted around on the surface as a result of convection currents (large-scale, heat-carrying flows) within the magma. The solid chunks collided

FIRE AND WATER When the Earth formed it had no oceans. Water vapour released by volcanic eruptions, such as this modern-day one on Hawaii, accumulated in the atmosphere until there was enough for clouds to form, then fall as rain. The rain filled depressions in the Earth's crust to create the oceans.

with each other, as well as with solid material, which poured out of massive volcanoes erupting at that time all over Earth. Gradually, the plates and volcanic material came together to form the nuclei of the continents. In the gaps between the chunks, where they had moved apart, new thinner crust formed through the cooling of upwelling magma. It was this crust that provided the base for the ocean basins.

The salty sea and early life

The water that first fell on Earth's surface was fresh. The primeval rains washed salt and other minerals from the rocks into the oceans, forming saline seawater. The salt content of the oceans eventually stabilised, and scientists speculate that this stability may have created perfect conditions for life to begin and then thrive.

The earliest evidence of life on Earth comes from 3.85 billion-year-old rocks. These contain a 'chemical fingerprint' – specifically, a particular mix of different forms of carbon – indicating that living organisms must have been present around the time the rocks were formed. In fact, some scientists think that life may have appeared as much as 500 million years earlier, but that it was wiped out by the meteorites, which were bombarding Earth at that time. Whatever the exact date when life started, it was at first slow to adapt and change; for almost 2 billion years – nearly half the planet's history – nothing more complex than bacteria existed. Yet these life-forms, once finally established in the oceans, set the pattern for Earth's future.

EARTH TODAY The tectonic plates that form Earth's crust are all on the move. At some boundaries, such as beneath the Atlantic, the plates are moving apart, and new crust forms as molten rock fills the gaps. In the north-east Pacific, old crust is being destroyed as the Pacific plate is forced beneath the Eurasian.

SUPERCONTINENT The Earth's continents may seem fixed, but they are constantly in motion. In the Late Permian Period, 255 million years ago, they were tightly packed together in a single supercontinent called Pangaea. The vast Panthalassa Ocean surrounded Pangaea, which in its turn bounded the shallower Tethys Sea.

BREAK-UP By the Late Jurassic, around 150 million years ago, the supercontinent of Pangaea had begun to break apart. Although still connected, two distinct smaller continents had started to form – Laurasia and Gondwana. As the gap between them grew, it filled with the embryonic Atlantic Ocean.

OUR WORLD EMERGES By the end of the Cretaceous, 65 million years ago, the world began to look like it does today, although the Tethys Sea still separated India from the rest of Asia. Also, sea levels were falling, due to global cooling locking up more water in the ice caps, and so more land was exposed.

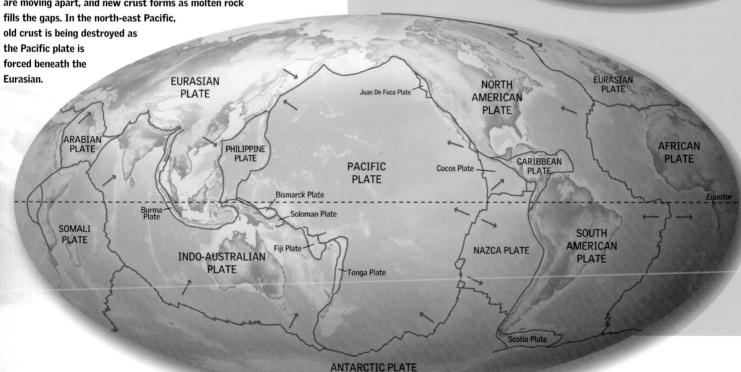

While the oceans' mineral content has remained stable, when life took hold it made a significant change to the dissolved gas content of seawater. Carbon dioxide was more abundant 3.85 billion years ago than it is now, while oxygen was non-existent. Dissolved oxygen began to appear around 3.5 billion years ago, and it was produced by a new group of life-forms – the cyanobacteria. These microbes, which still exist today, were the first living things on Earth to evolve photosynthesis, the process which harnesses energy from the Sun to produce sugars from water and carbon dioxide. Oxygen is a by-product of photosynthesis, and as cyanobacteria multiplied, the dissolved oxygen content of seawater grew.

By around 2.2 billion years ago, new life-forms, called eukaryotic organisms, appeared in the oceans. Although still single-celled, they were more complex than bacteria. Their cells had a nucleus and other structures that set them apart. One group of these new organisms also evolved structures, called chloroplasts, that could photosynthesise. They were the ancestors of single-celled algae and soon spread throughout the surface layers of the oceans. With their appearance, the amount of dissolved oxygen in the seawater rose again, leading to the evolution of new, oxygen-consuming organisms, including the ancestors of animals.

CHANGING OCEANS

ALTHOUGH THE OCEAN HAS BEEN A CONSTANT THROUGHOUT MOST OF EARTH'S HISTORY, and its volume and salt content have hardly changed at all, the shape and distribution of ocean basins has changed considerably. Even today, new areas of oceanic crust are being created while others are destroyed. This process is part of the phenomenon known as continental drift, which widens some oceans while shrinking others.

The Earth's crust is rather like the cracked shell of a boiled egg. It sits on top of a thick, partially molten layer known as the mantle. The crust is thickest beneath the continents. At the bottom of the oceans, it is thinner and contains the cracks where new crust is formed. These cracks allow molten rock to surge up from the mantle. As it does so, it gradually forces the cracks to open wider, pushing apart the plates (rigid areas of crust) on either side. Some of the molten rock spews out onto the seabed, where it quickly solidifies. The result is a deep, broken valley, bound on either side by submarine mountains, known as the mid-ocean ridge.

A large sector of the mid-ocean ridge today lies underneath the Atlantic Ocean, running from north to south for

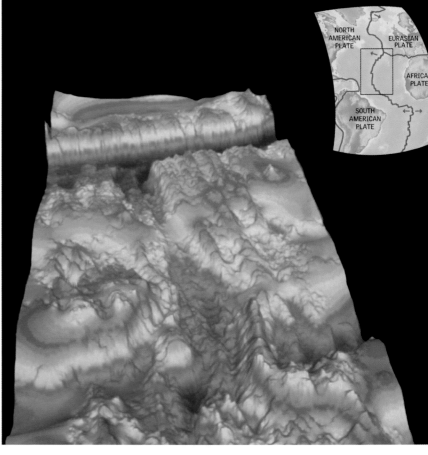

SEEN BY SONAR A huge mountain chain marks the plate boundary that snakes down the length of the Atlantic Ocean. Known as the Mid-Atlantic Ridge, it is one of the world's greatest mountain ranges, and is itself only part of the even greater global mid-ocean ridge that encircles most of the planet.

SPITZBERGEN ICE MELT In summer, the edges of the ice caps melt. In winter, the ice caps grow again as snow builds up on them and the sea surface becomes frozen. But climate change is threatening to destabilise this cycle. Rising temperatures have already caused the Arctic ice cap to retreat farther in the summer than ever before, and the losses have not been fully replaced by the winter freeze.

most of its length. Because of the ridge's existence, the Atlantic is becoming wider, pushing the Americas away from Europe and Africa at a rate of around 2.5 cm every year, which is about the same speed at which fingernails grow. By contrast, the Pacific Ocean is shrinking. Around its edges are so-called convergent boundaries, where oceanic crust is destroyed as it is forced beneath continents. These boundaries give rise to volcanic activity and are the main reason for the Pacific's 'Ring of Fire'.

These movements of the oceans are a sign of their relative ages. The Atlantic is comparatively young. It only began to form around 190 million years ago, during the Triassic Period. Evidence of this is seen today in similar dinosaur fossils found on either side of it. They were laid down at a time when Europe was still joined to North America and Africa to South America. The oldest crust in the Pacific formed earlier, in the zone once covered by the ocean that existed when all the modern continents were joined together in the supercontinent Pangaea.

While the Atlantic is relatively young, other, smaller branches of the World Ocean are even more recent additions, floored by continental rather than oceanic crust. The English Channel, for example, did not exist 12 000 years ago; nor did much of the North Sea or The Gulf between Arabia and Iran. During Earth's various ice ages, huge amounts of water were locked up in the expanded ice caps. As a result, sea levels around the world dropped, exposing vast areas of continental shelf – parts of the continental plates that are now underwater. At other times, the average temperature on Earth has been significantly higher than it is today. During those periods, sea levels were higher, too, and large areas of the continents were flooded by the ocean.

How the Mediterranean formed

While many seas have come and gone through changes in temperature, today's Mediterranean Sea was created as a result of geological forces. Just under 6 million years ago, the gap between Spain and North Africa closed completely, leaving the Mediterranean landlocked. Within a few thousand years, most of the sea had evaporated, forming huge tracts of salt-encrusted desert. This situation lasted for around half a million years. Then, about 5.4 million years ago, the Strait of Gibraltar reopened and water from the Atlantic came back in.

Despite its connection with the Atlantic, the water of the Mediterranean is saltier and it has less diverse marine life than the Atlantic. The reason for this is that the waters of the two hardly mix at all – the Strait of Gibraltar is only about 300 m deep and just 14 km wide at its narrowest point. This virtual separation also means that the Mediterranean has no significant tides. Its average tidal range is no more than a few centimetres, compared with more than 1 m on the Atlantic Ocean side of the Strait.

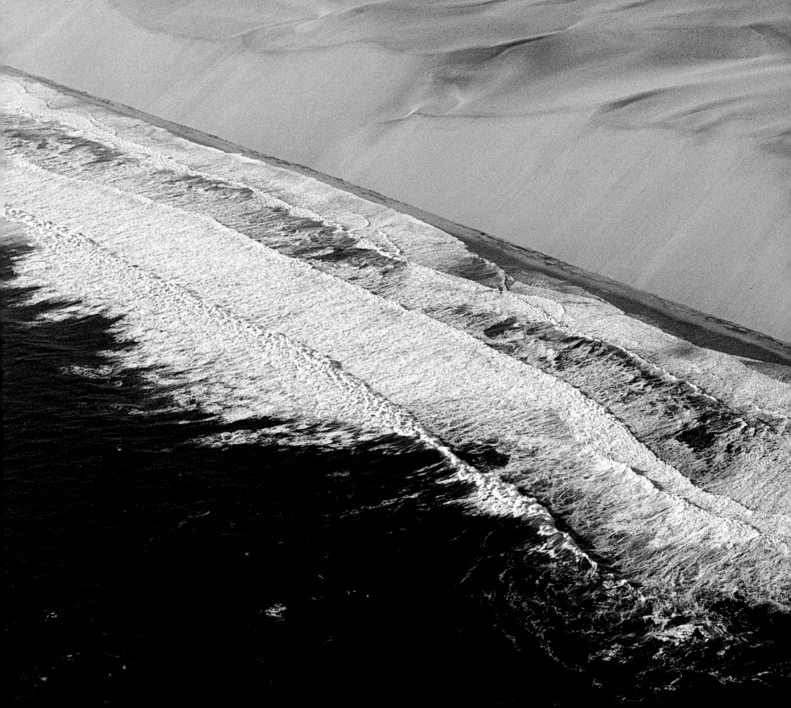

MIGHTY
CURRE

NTS

2

WATER IN THE OCEANS IS CONSTANTLY ON THE MOVE, transported by powerful currents that stream through the oceans like great rivers, moving heat and nutrients and mixing up the water from different regions of the Earth. Currents are most easily discerned where two meet and flow past or above and beneath one another. Their impact is felt not just in the sea, but also on land as they are the driving force behind much of the world's weather. Off the coast of Namibia, upwelling water along the west coast of Africa meets the icy Benguela Current travelling north from Antarctica. The clash between them forms great banks of fog (left). These roll in from the sea every night, bringing precious moisture to the coastal Namib Desert, a place where rain is almost unknown, and enabling life to survive.

RIVERS IN THE SEA

EVEN WHEN IT LOOKS PEACEFUL, THE OCEAN IS NEVER STILL. Currents continuously churn the waters both at the surface and far below. Some surface currents extend to a depth of over 1 km, others can stretch 1000 km wide. Their speeds vary, but the most powerful travel up to 200 km a day in places. Water moves over the seabed in massive rivers just as it does at the surface, but does so much more slowly, taking centuries rather than months to travel the length of an ocean.

The causes of ocean currents are complex, but surface currents are driven mainly by prevailing winds. Deep currents, which circulate in a vertical as well as horizontal direction, are driven by the rising and sinking of water in different parts of the world due to variations in temperature. Different currents also interact with and affect one another. On a global scale, they are parts of a single, interconnected system that has a profound effect on Earth's climate and on life in the sea.

Most major currents run through the open ocean, but smaller, more localised currents occur along coasts. Coastal currents form wherever prevailing winds blow from the shore, pushing surface water out to sea. As the surface water is driven away from the shore, cooler water wells up from below to replace it. That water is also pushed out to sea in its turn, and the cycle continues. As cooler water drawn up from the depths is usually rich in nutrients, coastal currents of this type support abundant life. Some of the world's most productive fisheries occur over them, including those of the North Sea and along the coasts of California, Peru and West Africa.

Surface currents

Surface currents follow the major wind belts that circle the globe: the north-east and south-east trade winds on either side of the Equator, the westerlies in the mid-latitudes and the polar easterlies. The friction caused by these winds blowing over the ocean surface makes the water beneath them move in the same direction, although at a slower speed. And even when the wind drops temporarily, the movement of the water continues, carried onwards by its own momentum.

Surface currents that move away from the Equator transport warm water from the topics to higher latitudes, where the water loses its heat to the atmosphere, producing a temperate climate. Surface currents that move from the polar and temperate regions towards the Equator transport cold water back to the tropics, where it absorbs heat from the Sun and the cycle starts again. While about two-thirds of global heat transport is by winds moving warm air around, the remaining third is by warm water currents.

A global network

Major warm surface currents include the Atlantic Gulf Stream and the Agulhas Current, which flows south along the east coast of Africa. These are the two fastest-flowing currents. Cold currents include the Peru and Benguela, which flow up from the Southern Ocean along the coasts of South America and West Africa, respectively. The world's largest current is the Antarctic Circumpolar Current (also known as the West Wind Drift), which circles Antarctica in an easterly direction and is the only current that travels all round the Earth without being deflected by land. Although it moves slowly, it carries more water than any other current – about 130 million m^3 per second, which is 150 times more water than all of the Earth's rivers combined.

Surface currents were the first to be identified and mapped. The Gulf Stream was described in the early 16th century by Spanish navigators exploring the Americas, and European sailors used it to speed their journeys home. According to legend, Christopher Columbus was inspired to

GOING WITH THE FLOW The coconut palm grows along sandy beaches and uses the ocean's surface currents to transport its light, buoyant seeds to new shores. The coconut can germinate after spending considerable time in seawater.

SURFACE CURRENTS Surface water moves horizontally in well-defined patterns, or currents. These follow in the wake of prevailing winds, but are modifed by the shapes of the ocean basins beneath them and by the Coriolis effect (see page 37). Within each ocean basin currents flow in large rotating loops, called gyres. Warm currents are shown in red and cold in blue.

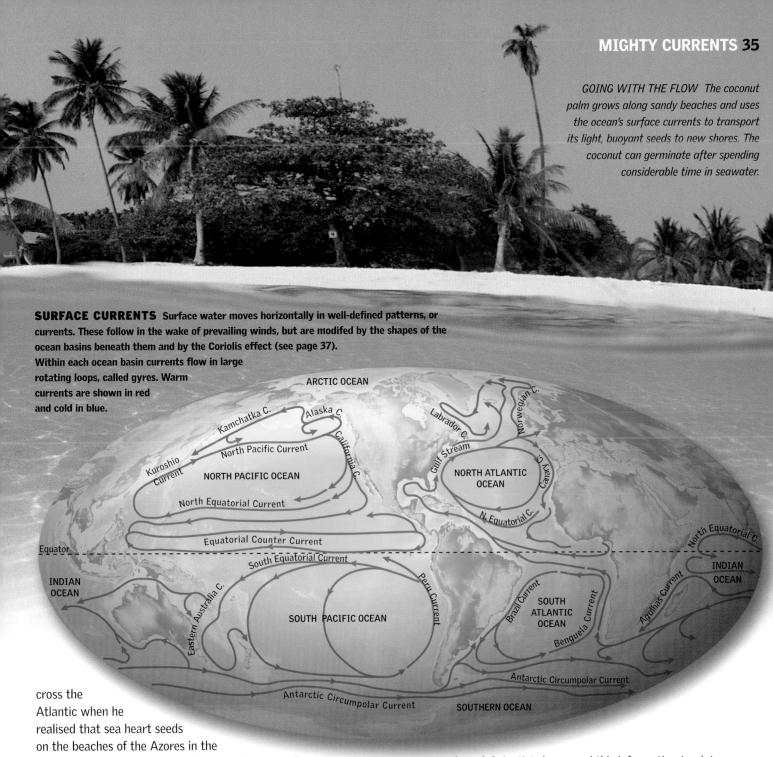

cross the Atlantic when he realised that sea heart seeds on the beaches of the Azores in the Atlantic must have been carried across the ocean from distant lands to the west. The sea heart is a vine that grows in the tropical forests of Costa Rica. Its seeds are carried by currents through the Caribbean, washing up around the Gulf of Mexico and Florida Keys. Some ride the Gulf Stream and North Atlantic currents to Europe, where they have been found not only in the Azores, but around the British Isles and as far north as Norway.

Of course, it is not just seeds that are carried by the currents. In 1992, a container ship carrying toys from China to Seattle lost some of its load in the North Pacific. Among the containers that fell overboard was one filled with brightly coloured plastic bath toys, some of which went on to make mammoth journeys. Between November 1992 and August 1993, more than 800 were found washed up along an 850 km stretch of Alaskan coastline, 15 000 km from the point where they went overboard. Scientists have used this information to plot the currents that must have carried them. Much of what we know about the ocean's surface currents comes from similar stories of lost or jettisoned cargo, together with the release of drift buoys, which scientists use to produce computer models of surface currents.

Currents have also transported people. In 1947, the Norwegian anthropologist Thor Heyerdahl and five colleagues set out from Callao, Peru, on a balsawood raft, the *Kon-Tiki,* to prove that people could have reached Polynesia from South America. After riding the currents for 101 days and travelling 6920 km, they arrived at the island of Raroia in the Tuamotu archipelago. Since then, archaeology and DNA evidence have shown that the Pacific peoples spread out from Indonesia, not South America, but they still knew how to navigate currents.

OCEAN DRIFTERS JELLYFISH TRAVEL THE WORLD BY CATCHING A RIDE ON THE CURRENTS.

They are well adapted to this drifting lifestyle, having no bone or thick muscles and being 95 per cent water. This makes them effectively one with their environment, and they can remain buoyant without having to expend precious energy on staying afloat. They are relatively weak swimmers and propel themselves through water in pursuit of food by contracting and expanding their bell-shaped bodies. When they gather in swarms, it is usually because they have been brought together by currents. Being at the mercy of the water, they are often pushed into bays, and many end their lives washed up and helpless on beaches.

Jellyfish belong to a group of simple animals called the cnidarians. Their closest relatives are sea anemones and corals. Like them, jellyfish have a mouth surrounded by tentacles, each armed with special stinging cells to stun and capture prey. Although they are soft-bodied and slow-moving, they have few natural predators as their stinging tentacles make them too dangerous for most animals to tackle. Also, being almost entirely water, they make a poor food source. But there is one creature that hunts jellyfish. The leatherback turtle, or luth, eats little else and rides the currents, following jellyfish wherever they go. In the North Atlantic large numbers of leatherbacks follow the Gulf Stream as far as Britain, where they feed on barrel jellyfish (below) and moon jellyfish off the coast of Wales.

JELLYFISH

VITAL STATISTICS

PHYLUM: Cnidaria CLASS: Scyphozoa
NUMBER OF SPECIES: Around 200
DISTRIBUTION: Worldwide
HABITAT: Open seawater at various depths
KEY FEATURE: Poisonous tentacles.
A few jellyfish are dangerous to humans.
The most notorious is the sea wasp, or box jellyfish,
whose sting can kill a human in minutes.

FULL CIRCLE

ALTHOUGH SURFACE CURRENTS ARE KEPT MOVING BY THE WIND, THEIR DIRECTION IS INFLUENCED BY THE EARTH'S ROTATION. They are deflected in a clockwise direction in the Northern Hemisphere, and anticlockwise in the Southern Hemisphere. This is known as the Coriolis effect: combined with the positions of continental land masses, it produces rotating systems of linked currents, called gyres. These great swirls of water occur in the subtropical regions, with smaller gyres in the Arctic regions.

Gyres – giant wheels

There are five major subtropical gyres, one each in the North and South Atlantic, the North and South Pacific and the Indian Ocean. Typical gyres consist of four main currents – two aligned roughly north-south and two east-west – that link up to form a continuous loop. The North Atlantic gyre, for example, consists of the Gulf Stream, the North Atlantic Current, the Canary Current and the North Equatorial Current.

Smaller gyres in the Arctic basins of the North Atlantic and Pacific are driven by the counterclockwise winds of the polar latitudes, so these flow in the opposite direction to the Northern Hemisphere subtropical gyres. Polar gyres do not exist in the Southern Hemisphere because there are no large landmasses to constrain the east-west currents in the Southern Ocean.

The water within a gyre is higher in the middle than at the edges. The combined forces of the wind, the Earth's rotation and friction within the water itself push the water at the centre upwards, forming a shallow-sloped mound about 2 m high. Although gyres turn like great wheels, they are not symmetrical. Because the Coriolis effect is stronger near the poles than near the Equator, the centre of a gyre, where the water is piled up highest, is in fact off-centre, and the currents flow deeper and faster on one side than the other. In the Northern Hemisphere, the western boundary currents – the Gulf Stream and the Pacific's Kuroshio – move fastest, an effect known as the western intensification.

The surface currents provide a system of linked highways that transport countless drifters – from microscopic plankton to larger animals such as jellyfish – on vast journeys, pursued by the creatures that feed on them. Some species follow the gyres all their lives. Blue sharks, for example, follow the North Atlantic gyre, heading northwards in summer and south in autumn as the northerly waters start to cool.

NORTH POLE

ROTATION OF EARTH

WESTERLIES

NORTH ATLANTIC GYRE

NORTH-EAST TRADE WINDS

THE CORIOLIS EFFECT

The Coriolis effect is a phenomenon caused by the rotation of the Earth, which turns in an easterly direction. The effect can be explained by imagining a missile fired from the North Pole aimed at point B; it will actually land at point A because of the movement of the Earth beneath it while it travels. In the same way, the Earth's rotation causes winds and ocean currents – which would otherwise move directly between the Equator and the Poles – to be deflected in a clockwise direction in the Northern Hemisphere and in an anticlockwise direction in the Southern Hemisphere. In the North Atlantic, the north-east trade winds at the Equator drive surface water westwards, while at higher latitudes the westerlies drive it in an easterly direction. Because these lateral movements of water are blocked by the continental landmasses, they turn northwards or southwards, creating the boundary currents of the North Atlantic gyre.

CURRENT CRUISERS Blue sharks migrate to new feeding grounds by riding the North Atlantic gyre.

OCEAN CONVEYOR BELT
In the North Atlantic, salty water cools and sinks, and creeps south towards the Antarctic. Deep water returns to the surface in the Indian and Pacific Oceans through upwelling, and flows back towards the Atlantic.

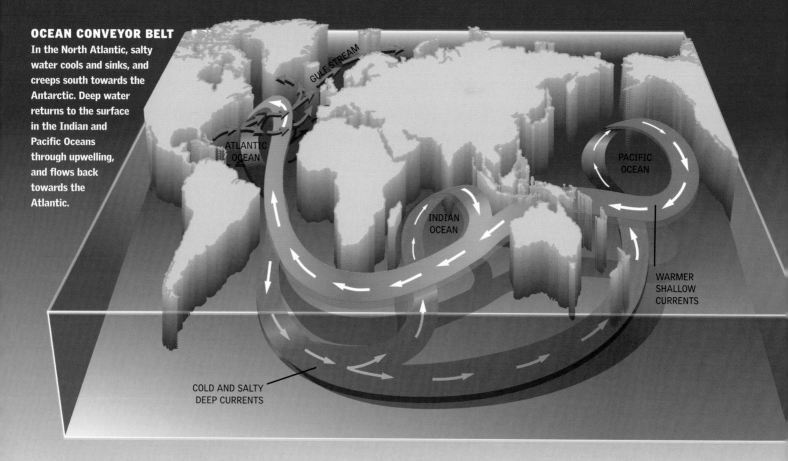

GULF STREAM

ATLANTIC OCEAN

PACIFIC OCEAN

INDIAN OCEAN

WARMER SHALLOW CURRENTS

COLD AND SALTY DEEP CURRENTS

DEEP-SEA CURRENTS

BELOW THE SURFACE LAYER OF THE OCEANS, A SERIES OF MUCH DEEPER CURRENTS FLOW AROUND THE PLANET. Unlike surface currents, which are caused and maintained by the wind, deep currents are driven by changes in water temperature and salinity. As water becomes saltier and cools, it sinks to the ocean floor, displacing water that is already there. Deep currents move extremely slowly, sometimes by as little as 1 m a day, and their routes are largely dictated by the shape of the seabed. As oceanographers currently understand it, these deep currents rise to the surface in places where they connect with surface currents, forming a continuous looping system that links the oceans. The system is known as the ocean conveyor belt, and it is powered by vast volumes of water sinking in the northern North Atlantic, acting like a great pump pushing water around the globe. A similar amount of bottom water is also generated around the Antarctic margin.

A slow, looping course

As the Gulf Stream travels north, water evaporates from the surface and its salinity increases. When this dense, salty water reaches the polar regions of the Atlantic, it encounters ice and rapidly cools and contracts, becoming so heavy that it plunges to the ocean floor, displacing warmer water as it goes. This mass of cold water, known as the North Atlantic Deep Water, inches southwards over the Atlantic seabed until it eventually reaches the continent of Antarctica, where it turns eastwards.

Directly south of Africa the conveyor belt splits in two. One branch spreads north-eastwards across the floor of the Indian Ocean; the other continues eastwards into the Pacific before it turns north. As the deep water mixes with warmer, less salty water, it wells up. In the middle of the Indian Ocean and in the North Pacific, the two branches of the conveyor belt reach the surface and join wind-blown currents travelling back towards the North Atlantic, where the cycle starts again. One complete circuit of the conveyor belt takes several centuries, and perhaps as long as 1000 years.

Threats to the conveyor belt

The ocean conveyor belt has existed since the end of the last Ice Age. It plays an important role in feeding and maintaining many surface currents, not least the Gulf Stream. It influences global weather patterns, and it brings nutrient-rich water up from the depths and redistributes it around the globe. Some scientists are worried that its existence may be threatened by global warming. A rise in temperatures that caused ice to melt at the poles would produce an increase in the amount of fresh water entering the oceans, reducing salinity levels so that cold water would be less likely to sink. This could cause the conveyor belt to break up, and if this happens, the consequences could be severe. One likely outcome would be the devastation of fisheries, affecting many fish species as well as the livelihoods of whole communities. The impact of changed currents on the world's weather could be even more far-reaching, although the effects are almost impossible for scientists to predict.

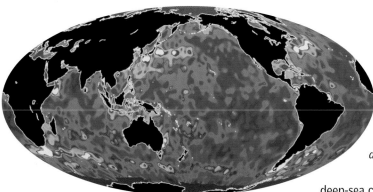

MAPPING THE OCEAN SURFACE
This satellite image shows the major surface currents represented by the yellow, red and white areas. Dark blue represents stable areas, such as at the centres of oceans.

Tracking currents

Because of the inaccessibility of the deep-water currents that make up the conveyor belt, scientists' models were until recently mainly theoretical, built from scraps of information obtained by dropping instruments from the sides of ships. Now, however, deep currents are monitored more closely using floats built to drift at set depths. These travel with the currents, popping up to the surface periodically to beam the information they have gathered to satellites, before sinking again.

The floats are as smooth as torpedoes, but they have an unwieldy name: Profiling Autonomous Lagrangian Circulation Explorer, or PALACE, floats. They can operate unattended for several years and trace precisely the direction and speed of deep-sea currents, giving oceanographers a glimpse of the workings of the depths that they could otherwise never hope to have. The hundreds in place in the Atlantic Ocean are providing a map of meandering trajectories that confirm theories on general patterns, but also throw up new questions about how deep-water currents behave.

In 1999, an international programme was launched to pepper the world's oceans with some 3000 PALACE floats. Called Argo, its aim was to gather information on ocean movements at various depths in real time. From the data it has already provided, scientists have been able to improve their climate models, which should enable them to make more accurate forecasts of future climate change.

THE SARGASSO SEA

Currents are affected by the submarine landscape, and this can create giant pockets of water that are largely unaffected by the ocean all around them. The most famous of these pockets is the Sargasso Sea. Hemmed in by the clockwise-moving North Atlantic gyre (see page 37), its weed-infested waters are slack and salty, and home to unique animal life, including fish and crabs. The occasional invasion of eddies from the Gulf Stream causes the weed to 'bloom' (below), like a desert after a storm.

Sargasso
Sea

THE GULF STREAM WAS FIRST DOCUMENTED IN 1513

by the Spanish navigator Juan Ponce de Léon. On April 22 of that year, while crossing the Straits of Florida, Leon wrote in his log of 'a current more powerful than the wind'.

IT IS THE WORLD'S FASTEST-MOVING OCEAN CURRENT

with a maximum speed of 2 m/sec at the surface. At a depth of more than 1 km its speed slows to 10 cm/sec.

FACTS

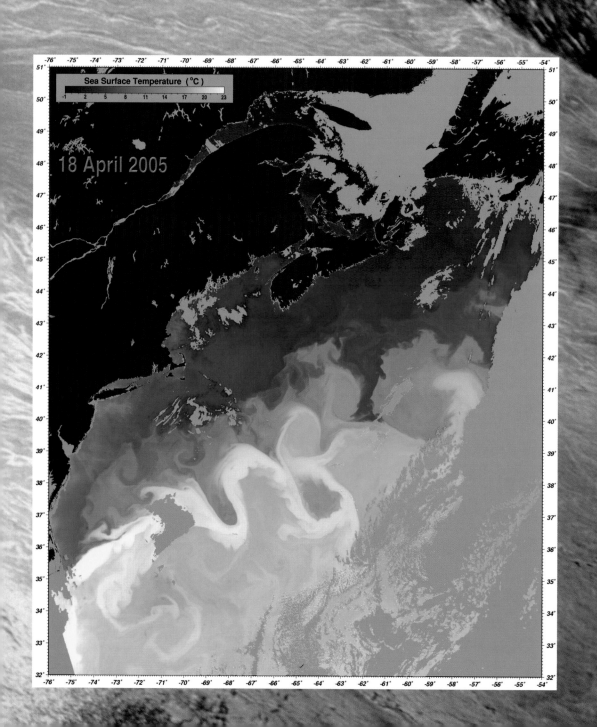

Sea Surface Temperature (°C)

-1   2   5   8   11   14   17   20   23

18 April 2005

THIS MIGHTY SURFACE CURRENT CARRIES WARM, TROPICAL WATER ACROSS THE NORTH ATLANTIC TO EUROPE. Its flow rate is hundreds of times that of the Amazon, and its impact is massive. The warm waters it brings raise the sea temperature by a full 10°C, affecting the climate of the whole of western Europe.

The Gulf Stream takes its name from the Gulf of Mexico, where it begins. At the Florida Channel, the warm surface waters leaving the Gulf are joined by branches of the North Equatorial Current, itself a mighty river of seawater and part of the North Atlantic gyre (see page 37). This combined mass of water travels up the eastern seaboard of the United States, but is separated from it by the tail end of the cold, southward-flowing Labrador Current. Off Newfoundland, the Gulf Stream veers out into the open Atlantic and travels across the ocean towards Europe.

THE GULF STREAM

Just west of the British Isles the Gulf Stream splits in two. The northern branch (known as the North Atlantic Current) continues past the northern British Isles towards Scandinavia and the Arctic. As it does so it begins to peter out, losing dense, heavy water to the deep. This joins the North Atlantic Deep Water, part of the ocean conveyor belt (see pages 38-39). The southern branch of the Gulf Stream turns and heads south-eastwards to join the Canary Current.

The Gulf Stream is one of the most powerful surface currents in the world. At its peak, off Cape Hatteras, North Carolina, it moves at a rate of 80 million m³ per second. By comparison, the combined rate of all the rivers flowing into the Atlantic is barely 0.6 million m³ per second.

A dynamic system

While the Gulf Stream can be visualised as a gigantic river, its true structure is far more complex. Along its western edge huge meanders develop and fill with cold water from the Labrador Current. These sometimes become pinched off, forming cold-water eddies that may persist for years. The bulges between meanders fill with warm water. If they pinch off, they become

WARM WATER ON THE MOVE The Gulf Stream flows northwards along the east coast of the USA and then heads north-eastwards across the Atlantic. From space (left) a clear boundary is visible between the warm, faster-flowing water of the Gulf Stream (in the lower half) and the calmer, cold coastal water. The current develops a looping, meandering path as it heads into the Atlantic, and complex eddies develop along its western boundary.

warm-water eddies, which can be hundreds of kilometres across and carry warm water far from where it would normally be found. Their arrival in an area can impact on the local weather.

As well as changing over time at its edges, the Gulf Stream varies in relative width and speed along its length. It is fastest and narrowest nearest its source. As it passes through the narrow Straits of Florida, it is just 80 km across but moves at up to 16 km/h. Farther north, it is slower but significantly wider – by the time it reaches the ocean off New York, it is around 480 km across. Its speed in the open Atlantic, where it is blown by prevailing southwesterly winds, rarely exceeds 1 km/h.

The Gulf Stream is at its maximum temperature as it leaves the Gulf of Mexico, reaching 27°C. This drops as the current travels north and east, although it retains enough heat to warm the coast of Europe from Spain to Norway.

Moderating the weather

The effect of all this moving water is felt on both sides of the Atlantic. The east coast of Florida, and the south-east in particular, owes its favourable climate almost entirely to the Gulf Stream. The warm waters make winters here much milder than they would otherwise be. Summers, by contrast, are cooler than in the other south-eastern states.

Farther north, the effects of the Gulf Stream are most significant offshore. The cool waters that hug the eastern coast of North America meet the Gulf Stream at a boundary known as the Cold Wall, many kilometres from land. Water temperatures change suddenly along this boundary. Near the northern end of the Cold Wall thick blankets of fog often form. Among seafarers, these dense, persistent fogs are notorious, the worst being those around the Grand Banks off Newfoundland, which, over the years, have claimed dozens of ships.

On the other side of the Atlantic, the Gulf Stream brings warmth to western Europe, its waters bathing the coasts and keeping ports ice-free all year round. As the current comes into

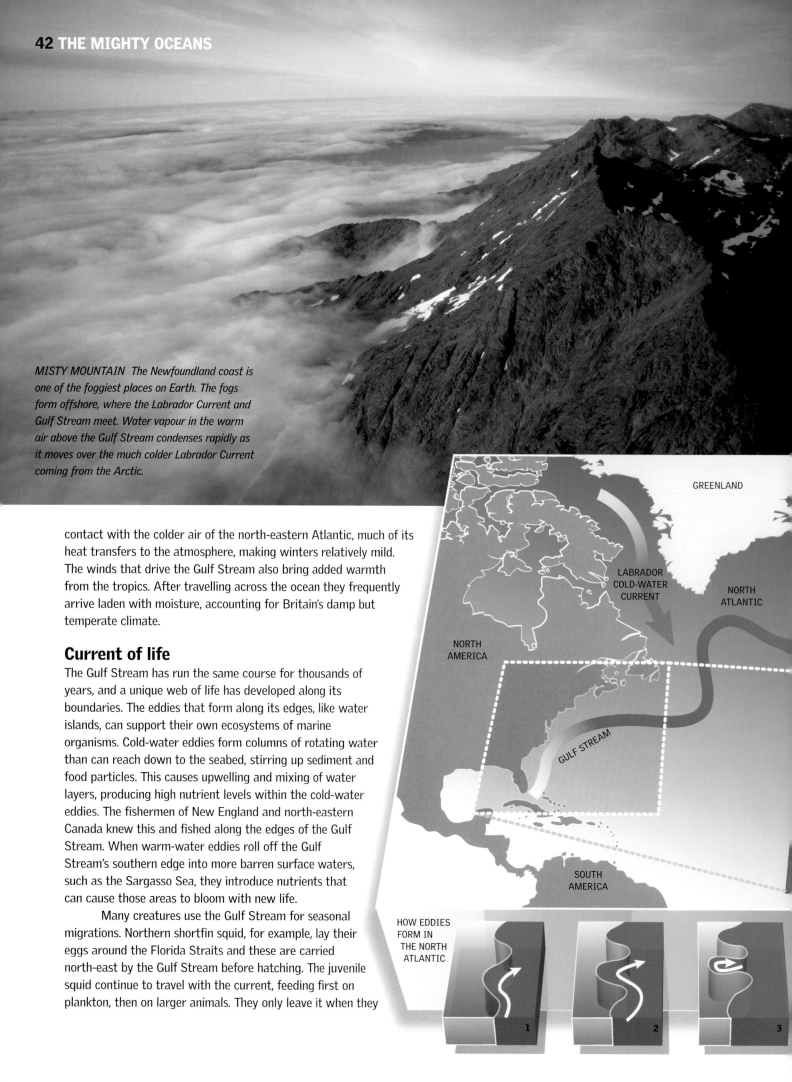

MISTY MOUNTAIN The Newfoundland coast is one of the foggiest places on Earth. The fogs form offshore, where the Labrador Current and Gulf Stream meet. Water vapour in the warm air above the Gulf Stream condenses rapidly as it moves over the much colder Labrador Current coming from the Arctic.

GREENLAND

LABRADOR
COLD-WATER
CURRENT

NORTH
ATLANTIC

NORTH
AMERICA

GULF STREAM

SOUTH
AMERICA

HOW EDDIES
FORM IN
THE NORTH
ATLANTIC

1

2

3

contact with the colder air of the north-eastern Atlantic, much of its heat transfers to the atmosphere, making winters relatively mild. The winds that drive the Gulf Stream also bring added warmth from the tropics. After travelling across the ocean they frequently arrive laden with moisture, accounting for Britain's damp but temperate climate.

Current of life

The Gulf Stream has run the same course for thousands of years, and a unique web of life has developed along its boundaries. The eddies that form along its edges, like water islands, can support their own ecosystems of marine organisms. Cold-water eddies form columns of rotating water than can reach down to the seabed, stirring up sediment and food particles. This causes upwelling and mixing of water layers, producing high nutrient levels within the cold-water eddies. The fishermen of New England and north-eastern Canada knew this and fished along the edges of the Gulf Stream. When warm-water eddies roll off the Gulf Stream's southern edge into more barren surface waters, such as the Sargasso Sea, they introduce nutrients that can cause those areas to bloom with new life.

Many creatures use the Gulf Stream for seasonal migrations. Northern shortfin squid, for example, lay their eggs around the Florida Straits and these are carried north-east by the Gulf Stream before hatching. The juvenile squid continue to travel with the current, feeding first on plankton, then on larger animals. They only leave it when they

GULF STREAM

BRITISH ISLES

EUROPE

NORTH AMERICA

EDDIES

TEMPERATURE RANGE OF THE GULF STREAM

reach adulthood, travelling through the colder water down the North American east coast to Florida, where the cycle starts again.

Other young animals ride the length of the Gulf Stream. After hatching on Florida's beaches, young loggerhead and green turtles make straight for its warm waters, swimming frantically until they leave the more dangerous coastal waters behind. Once in the Gulf Stream they stay there, the young loggerheads feeding on invertebrates such as crabs and mussels among the flotsam, and the green turtles in more open water.

An uncertain future

Without the Gulf Stream, western Europe would be a far colder, bleaker place. London lies on the same latitude as central Canada and northern Mongolia. The fear among many scientists is that global warming could disrupt the Gulf Stream, causing Europe's climate to chill. If carbon dioxide emissions continue to rise as they have been, the greenhouse effect will worsen, leading to increased rainfall and melting polar ice. This added influx of cold, fresh water into the northern North Atlantic, particularly via the Labrador Current, could conceivably cause the Gulf Stream to change direction, and possibly shut down its northern branch completely. The result would be a Europe seized by Siberian winters, with icebergs floating as far south as the English Channel. Of course, such a scenario might never come to pass, and if it does, it is unlikely to be in our lifetimes.

RICH PICKINGS Cold, nutrient-rich water along the Grand Banks, off Newfoundland, supports one of the world's richest fisheries (above left).

SUBTROPICAL BRITAIN Because of the warmth brought by the Gulf Stream, gardeners in the Scilly Isles, to the west of Cornwall, can grow plants normally found only in much more southerly latitudes (above).

GULF STREAM EDDIES Although the direction of the Gulf Stream across the Atlantic is relatively constant, meanders form along its boundary with the cold Labrador Current (1). Bulges develop and fill with either cold or warm water (2). Meanders are gradually pinched off by the current (3). As the boundary re-forms, eddies begin rotating and spin out into the waters north or south of the current (4). Gulf Stream eddies can persist for up to five years before finally losing momentum and being absorbed into the waters around them.

COLD & WET

EL NINO

THE WORLD'S WEATHER IS INTIMATELY TIED TO THE OCEAN CURRENTS, as is seen in the phenomenon known as the El Niño-Southern Oscillation. The term El Niño refers to a body of warm water that gradually builds up in the western Pacific and which, in some years, travels back across the ocean towards America. In years when an abnormally large El Niño occurs, surface currents and airflows in the equatorial region of the Pacific temporarily reverse direction, producing dramatic changes in the region's weather patterns.

El Niños were first recognised by fishermen along the Pacific coast of South America. There, the main effect of the arrival of El Niño is a rapid warming of surface waters, leading to a sudden decline in fish stocks. In normal years this lasts for some two to three months. The name El Niño, 'Boy Child' in Spanish, refers to the fact that the phenomenon usually occurs around Christmas.

A system in reverse

The normal circulation pattern in the Pacific region is produced by an area of high atmospheric pressure over the eastern Pacific, where the California and Peru Currents merge into the Equatorial Current (see pages 34-35), and a low-pressure area over the western side, above Indonesia and northern Australia. The high-pressure area causes a strong surface airflow towards the low-pressure area in the west, and this combines with the trade winds to drive the South Equatorial Current westwards, piling up warm water around Indonesia. Some of this water flows back eastwards as the Equatorial Counter-Current. In normal years, sea levels around Indonesia are about 50 cm higher than they are off Ecuador.

Every few years, the pressure difference between the east and west Pacific regions breaks down temporarily and the trade winds in the central and western Pacific relax. This event,

TWO FACES OF EL NINO The El Niño event of 1997-8 caused terrific storms to batter the coast of southern California (above), with rainfall exceeding double the normal amount. While California was drenched, Tasmania experienced drought and bush fires (above right) and far lower rainfall than in normal years.

known as the Southern Oscillation, produces a sudden reversal in wind and water flow. The warm water that is being pressed up against Indonesia surges back across the Pacific as a greatly enlarged Equatorial Counter-Current. This gigantic body of warm water has a surface area one and a half times the size of the USA and contains a vast reserve of heat. It would require the energy from 1 million 10-megaton hydrogen bombs (a 10-megaton bomb is roughly equivalent to 770 Hiroshima bombs) to heat an equivalent amount of seawater to the same degree. Being less dense than normal seawater, the warm water floats rather like an iceberg, mostly submerged but protruding up to 1.5 m above the surface of the surrounding ocean.

An extreme El Niño leads to a drop in sea level and water temperature off Indonesia, but raises water temperature in the eastern Pacific by as much as 8°C, shutting down the cold South American upwelling. Rainfall in the western Pacific, which is normally driven by the piled-up warm water and trade winds, also reduces. Instead, rain falls in greater quantities over the open ocean and eastern Pacific coasts.

This change in rainfall patterns has serious consequences for countries around the Pacific. The strength of El Niño varies from year to year, but during particularly bad occurrences there will be floods down the eastern Pacific rim and droughts in the countries round the western rim. The worst El Niño on record began in 1997 and lasted into early 1998. It caused terrible storms and flooding in California, Mexico, Ecuador, Peru and Argentina. On the other side of the Pacific, severe drought led

HOT & DRY

A NORMAL YEAR Low-pressure systems form over Indonesia and northern Australia in the west Pacific, and high pressure dominates over the coast of Peru in the east. Regular trade winds drive the warm surface waters of the Pacific westwards. This build-up of warm water generates convective storms that keep northern Australia and Indonesia inundated with rain. In the eastern Pacific, cold water wells up to replace that lost from the surface, bringing with it the nutrients to support a food chain that sustains huge shoals of fish.

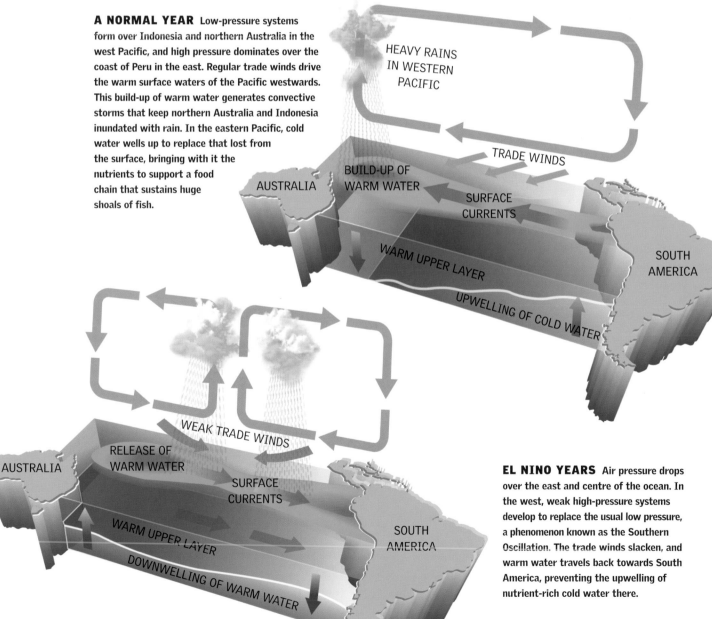

HEAVY RAINS IN WESTERN PACIFIC

TRADE WINDS

AUSTRALIA

BUILD-UP OF WARM WATER

SURFACE CURRENTS

WARM UPPER LAYER

UPWELLING OF COLD WATER

SOUTH AMERICA

WEAK TRADE WINDS

AUSTRALIA

RELEASE OF WARM WATER

SURFACE CURRENTS

WARM UPPER LAYER

DOWNWELLING OF WARM WATER

SOUTH AMERICA

EL NINO YEARS Air pressure drops over the east and centre of the ocean. In the west, weak high-pressure systems develop to replace the usual low pressure, a phenomenon known as the Southern Oscillation. The trade winds slacken, and warm water travels back towards South America, preventing the upwelling of nutrient-rich cold water there.

EL NINO ON THE MOVE

These computer-enhanced satellite images show the development and course of the 1997 El Niño. Red and white areas indicate warm water, purple/dark red indicates cold water and green represents normal conditions.

JANUARY 1997

At the start of the El Niño, the trade winds weaken and warm water (the large red area) begins to travel east across the Pacific Ocean towards South America. At this stage it has not developed into an abnormal event.

JUNE 1997

Five months later and the full force of El Niño is being felt. The small patch of red has developed into a thick streak of warm water (white area with red outline). This has made its way eastwards and is piling up against the northern coast of South America, preventing the upwelling of cold water there. The first effects of the change are felt as fish stocks start to crash off Peru.

NOVEMBER 1997

The warm surface water has now built up to such an extent that it has forced its way northward as far as Vancouver. In its wake, it has brought unusually wet weather and will soon trigger violent storms. On the other side of the ocean, where the surface water has become a lot cooler (the purple area), rainfall has dropped off considerably and some places are seeing the signs of drought.

to forest fires raging through Sumatra and Borneo. Mongolia baked in temperatures of 42°C.

Although it is centred around the Pacific Ocean, the El Niño-Southern Oscillation has a knock-on effect on the weather worldwide. During 1997 and 1998, as a direct result of the ongoing El Niño, massive storms battered Central Europe, causing many rivers in Poland and the Czech Republic to break their banks. Kenya suffered uncharacteristic flooding, while cyclones struck Madagascar.

The effects of an extreme El Niño can linger for several years. The 1982-3 El Niño was so massive that a sizeable chunk of warm water travelling eastwards on the north side of the Equator ricocheted off the North American continent and travelled back across the Pacific in a north-westerly direction. It was still in evidence ten years later in the ocean east of Japan.

Mirror image

El Niño years are sometimes followed by an opposite oscillation called La Niña ('Girl Child'). During La Niña, surface temperatures in the central and eastern Pacific drop significantly below normal as more cold, deep water than usual wells up there. The effect on global weather is the opposite of El Niño. In places where conditions were abnormally mild during an El Niño, they become abnormally harsh. Where there was drought, storms occur; where it was abnormally wet, it becomes arid.

Like those of El Niño, the effects of La Niña are most strongly felt from December to

March. During the La Niña of 1998-9, rainfall in Australia was far higher than normal. India experienced unusually heavy monsoon rains, and wetter than average conditions were felt as far west as southern Africa. Another consequence of La Niña is that the polar jet stream moves farther south, so winter in the north-western and upper mid-western US states was even colder than usual. At the same time, the subtropical jet stream weakened, causing less rain to fall in the Gulf of Mexico and south-western USA. The subtropical jet stream normally drives prevailing westerly winds. With this barrier temporarily down, hurricanes rolling in from the Atlantic met far less resistance than usual. Florida and the Caribbean islands were battered. The 1998 hurricane season was the most deadly in 200 years.

Oscillation cycles in other oceans

Although the El Niño-Southern Oscillations are the best known, other major oscillations exist. The Pacific Decadal Oscillation occurs in the North Pacific and has two distinct phases. In one phase, the waters off the western USA are particularly warm, while those in the western and middle regions of the North Pacific are cooler than average. In the other phase the opposite occurs. The sea along the western coast of North America cools, while the waters out to sea get warmer. The cycle of change between the phases is slow, and the effects last for years. Warm waters persisted off the western USA from 1977-97. As the 1990s drew to a close, conditions returned to those that had prevailed in 1976 and for almost three decades before that.

The Atlantic Ocean has its own slow cycle of change, the North Atlantic Oscillation. This also has two distinct phases. In one phase – the phase we are in now – atmospheric pressure over the Arctic is lower than average. This has the effect of raising sea temperatures off north-west Europe and the eastern USA, making winters there milder. In the other phase, sea temperatures are higher and winters milder around Greenland and eastern Canada. Each phase lasts for several decades, although the tempo is irregular, making it hard to know when the next switch will come.

The other major surface temperature cycle is the Antarctic Circumpolar Wave. This consists of two areas of relatively warm water separated by two areas of cold water. The Wave travels westwards, but because it is embedded in the immense Antarctic Circumpolar Current it is also carried eastwards, taking eight years to complete a circuit of Antarctica. It affects weather in all three southern continents.

AFRICA UNDERWATER In 1997, Kenya suffered torrential rains as the world's weather felt the knock-on effects of the 1997-8 El Niño.

PURPLE HAZE Drought caused by the 1997 El Niño led to forest fires raging out of control across Indonesia. Neighbouring countries found themselves enveloped by the smoke. In Malaysia's capital, Kuala Lumpur, it blocked out the Sun (below).

MONITORING EL NIÑO

Although an El Niño event occurs every few years, researchers are unable to predict their length and severity, although they can give probabilities for the possible effects. Monitoring techniques are improving, however, and scientists have increasingly sophisticated tools at their disposal. Data from previous El Niños and the phases in between has been fed into supercomputers to produce precise climate models. These can say with some accuracy when to expect an El Niño – climate models predicted the severe El Niño of 1998. Other methods use data as it is gathered to provide an early warning. Staff at NASA's Space Flight Center have found that the microscopic algae known as phytoplankton provide a good indicator. These tiny organisms form coloured clouds that show up like dye in the Pacific currents. As conditions change, the clouds indicate changes in the currents. By watching them, NASA's scientists can detect the onset of an El Niño or La Niña a month before it is picked up by more traditional methods.

WAVE PO

WER 3

THE TIP OF A LIGHTHOUSE PEEPS OUT AS STORM WAVES POUND THE COAST AT NEWLYN IN CORNWALL. Sticking out like a toe in the water, the Cornish peninsula bears the full brunt of Atlantic storms. But even in the calmest of weather, waves lap the world's shores. Many waves start their lives far out to sea, created and nurtured by the winds. As waves build, they carry enormous energy – a single metre of wave front can contain over 100 kW, enough to power the average house for almost a week. Their assault on the land is never ending. Waves carve our cliffs and rocky coastlines, and they pile up the pebbles and sand that form our beaches – or wash them away. In places they are rapidly eroding our coasts. Over the last century, an estimated 76 million m^3 of rock have been lost to the sea from the Holderness coast of East Yorkshire.

HOW WAVES FORM

THE BIGGEST WAVES EVER OFFICIALLY RECORDED AT SEA smashed into USS *Ramapo*, an oil-transport ship of the US Navy, in February 1933. They measured 34 m from trough to peak – higher than the dome of St Paul's Cathedral in London. Not surprisingly, they occurred during a storm in the Pacific, which because of its vastness allows waves to build up to huge sizes that are less likely in smaller oceans.

The source of all ocean waves is the wind. The harder the wind blows, and the longer it blows, the bigger the waves become. Another important factor in determining the size of waves is the expanse of sea over which the wind is blowing – a distance called the 'fetch'. That is why waves in a big ocean like the Pacific or the Atlantic can reach far greater dimensions than the biggest waves created in the more confined waters of, say, the Mediterranean or Gulf of Mexico. In the Pacific, the fetch can be thousands of kilometres long, so there is plenty of room for waves to acquire more and more energy from the wind as they move along – and thus achieve their fearsome size. Only in the Southern Ocean, where the wind can literally blow right around the Earth, are even larger waves created.

Wave creation

If no wind has blown over an area of ocean for several days, its surface can be almost flat. When a breeze starts, first to form are tiny so-called capillary waves. These have an amplitude (the vertical distance between peaks and troughs) of just a few millimetres, and their wave length (the distance between

BLOWING A GALE The Southern Ocean has the world's roughest seas. Frequent storms and almost constant wind whip its surface into a mass of white-capped waves, making conditions tough for ships but great for albatrosses, which ride the updrafts from their crests. The heights of South Georgia loom above the waves.

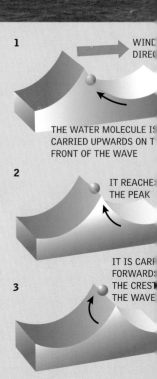

HOW WAVES MOVE FORWARDS

Although a large wave can travel for thousands of kilometres across an ocean, what actually moves forwards is not water, but energy. Water particles at the surface of an ocean do no more than move in a circle as a wave passes by. The forward transmission of energy occurs through particles of water near the ocean surface oscillating backwards and forwards. Particles first absorb kinetic energy in the direction of the waves from other particles behind them. They then move forwards and pass on the energy to particles in front of them. At the same time, there is a linked up-and-down oscillation of the particles. Putting the two oscillations together, each particle describes a circle, starting by moving predominantly upwards on the front face of a wave (1), then forwards at the crest of the wave (2 and 3), then downwards on the back of a wave (4 and 5) and, finally, backwards through the trough (6). This circular motion of the water is why, if you wade out where large waves are passing through, you feel yourself carried up and then forwards as each wave approaches, then down and finally backwards as it passes by.

1 WIND
DIREC[...]

THE WATER MOLECULE IS
CARRIED UPWARDS ON T[...]
FRONT OF THE WAVE

2 IT REACHE[...]
THE PEAK

3 IT IS CAR[...]
FORWARD[...]
THE CRES[...]
THE WAVE

successive peaks) is no more than a few centimetres. Capillary waves form through frictional effects between moving air molecules and the sea's surface. The energy of some of the air molecules is transferred to the water molecules, and this energy is then transmitted forward on the water surface through small, circular motions of the water particles (see box, below).

As the wind increases, more energy is transferred to the water as the moving air presses against the raised wavelets. Over time, this has the effect of raising the height of the waves and moving them forwards faster, increasing the distance between the wave peaks. Quite quickly, the sea surface is thrown into a series of waves with an amplitude of some tens of centimetres and a wavelength of several metres. This sea state is called a chop, or 'choppy sea'.

Stormy seas and ocean swell

With a wind blowing at storm force for an hour or two, a chop can be transformed into a highly turbulent sea, with some waves reaching heights of a metre or so. But in these circumstances the sea surface generally does not consist of regularly sized and spaced waves. More often it is chaotic, with the height and distance between waves varying considerably. The reason for this is a phenomenon called wave interference.

Usually, over a large area where waves are being generated, the wind will blow in varying strengths and directions in different places. This sets up many different wave trains – all of varying sizes, speeds and directions – which then combine. Where the peaks of two waves happen to coincide as they pass by each other, an extra large wave is momentarily created. Where the peak of one wave temporarily coincides with the trough of another, a wave smaller than its neighbours forms. Hence the confused and agitated appearance that results where several wave trains combine in a stormy sea. This is often heightened by some waves breaking and foaming at their peaks to create whitecaps, or sea horses.

Conversely, at a distance from the wave-generation area – perhaps several hundred kilometres away – a quite different pattern is seen. As different wave trains migrate away from the stormy area, they are automatically sorted by size and speed. First to arrive at the remote area are the largest, longest, fastest-moving wave trains, then those that are slightly smaller and slower-moving and so on. The overall result is a long-lasting series of regularly spaced waves, called a swell. The waves in a swell generally have heights of up to a few metres and wavelengths from about 10 m to hundreds of metres. On a boat in the open ocean, a swell is experienced as a regular rocking motion, repeating about once every 10 to 30 seconds.

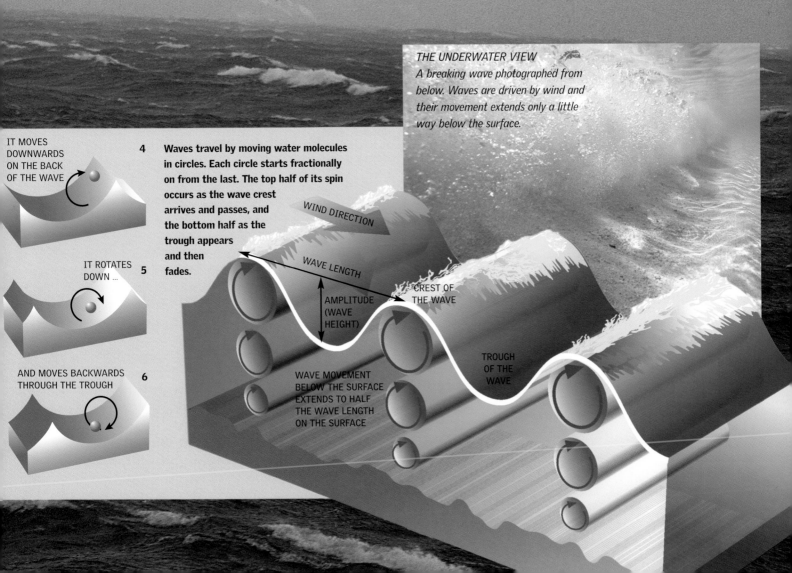

THE UNDERWATER VIEW
A breaking wave photographed from below. Waves are driven by wind and their movement extends only a little way below the surface.

IT MOVES DOWNWARDS ON THE BACK OF THE WAVE

4 Waves travel by moving water molecules in circles. Each circle starts fractionally on from the last. The top half of its spin occurs as the wave crest arrives and passes, and the bottom half as the trough appears and then fades.

IT ROTATES DOWN ... **5**

AND MOVES BACKWARDS THROUGH THE TROUGH **6**

WIND DIRECTION

WAVE LENGTH

AMPLITUDE (WAVE HEIGHT)

CREST OF THE WAVE

WAVE MOVEMENT BELOW THE SURFACE EXTENDS TO HALF THE WAVE LENGTH ON THE SURFACE

TROUGH OF THE WAVE

Freak waves

Fierce storms can create freak or rogue waves through the process of two or more very large waves interacting to produce a short-lived enormous one. In 2004, the European Space Agency (ESA) made a study into these waves, using satellite photographs of the ocean surface. What they found astonished everybody. Far from being rare, freak waves occurred with surprising frequency. Photographs taken over a three-week period showed no fewer than ten giant waves, each with an amplitude of 25 m or more.

One instance of a freak wave being observed at close quarters occurred on New Year's Day in 1995, when a 26 m high wave was measured passing under the Draupner Gas Platform in the North Sea. Such waves are now recognised as a threat to shipping. In 2000, for example, an inquiry into the fate of the *Derbyshire*, a British-owned bulk carrier that disappeared off Japan in 1980, concluded that a wave had probably cracked the ship open and flooded it. Investigations into such sinkings have often been cursory, with the cause usually put down as 'bad weather', but according to experts at the ESA freak waves have almost certainly been to blame in many cases.

The biggest rogue waves ever recorded are still the series of 34 m monsters that shivered USS *Ramapo* in the Pacific on February 7, 1933. An officer on board the ship calculated that the distance between the waves was about 340 m, and that they were travelling at about 83 km/h (45 knots). The crew of the *Ramapo* lived to tell the tale because the ship was relatively short, with a length of just 146 m, and managed to ride through these long wavelength ocean mountains relatively comfortably. The effect on a much larger modern-day tanker could have been catastrophic.

MORNING GLORY These wave structures, known as horsetails, form as spray from breaking waves is blown back out to sea by strong breezes. Coastal breezes that blow out to sea occur at night, when the ocean is warmer than the land, and persist into the early morning hours before changing direction as the land warms up. These were photographed off Australia.

ARRIVAL ON SHORE

AS WAVES APPROACH A COAST, THEY GROW LARGER AND BECOME MORE TIGHTLY BUNCHED. The reason for this change in their structure is the change in water depth. Far away from shore, waves are unaffected by depth, because the circular motions in the water as a wave passes by occur only to a limited distance underwater. For example, with waves spaced 10 m apart, movement occurs underwater down to a depth of only about 5 m.

But as a wave approaches a shore and the water becomes shallower, the seafloor begins to affect these motions and slows the wave down through the effects of friction. The shallower the water becomes, the more the waves are slowed, and the distance between them – their wave length – decreases. Each wave is still carrying the same amount of energy, however, and as a result its amplitude (height) increases.

Although waves may arrive at a coast from many different directions, when seen from a beach, they nearly always seem to be approaching straight on to the shore. The reason for this is a phenomenon called wave refraction, which occurs when the waves hit shallower coastal water where the underlying shore is sloping upwards towards the beach. As a wave front (the horizontal line of a wave crest) hits this zone at an angle, the end that meets the shallower water first is slowed down, while the other end keeps moving at the same speed. The effect on the whole wave front is to bend it as it rises up the sloping shore towards the coastline. By the time it is about to break on the beach, the wave front is nearly parallel to the coastline.

Swash, backwash and rip currents

As a wave progresses up a shore, the friction at its base becomes so powerful that the top of the wave begins to overtake the bottom. Eventually, gravity drags the overhanging water crest

CLIFF HANGER Over time, waves eat away at cliffs, causing them to crumble – as here on the Chesapeake Bay in Maryland, USA. Man-made defences such as seawalls may halt the process, but these have to be constantly maintained to remain effective.

HARNESSING WAVE POWER

The energy within waves is enormous, even on calm days. The World Energy Council estimates that by capturing this power we could generate twice as much electricity as we currently use, yet at present wave power accounts for only a tiny fraction of the electricity produced. This is mainly because of the high costs of building wave power stations. Once they are up and running, however, the fuel is endless and free. This station on the Scottish island of Islay works by converting wave energy into wind. As incoming waves rise inside a concrete chamber, they compress the air above them, forcing it through a long tube containing wind turbines. When they fall, they drag the air back in, driving the turbines (which rotate in the same direction regardless of air flow) for a second time.

down and the wave breaks. Then, after it has crashed on the shore, its water carries on up the beach until stopped by gravity. Some of this 'swash' seeps into the beach itself, but the rest flows back towards the sea and into the base of the next incoming wave. This returning water is known as backwash.

On some beaches, swash tends to gather and form pools at specific locations before returning to the sea. This causes a potentially dangerous rip current, like a river of seawater flowing back into the sea. The water from the swash is funnelled back through channels on the seabed, sometimes travelling hundreds of metres offshore. Rip currents – or rip tides as they are sometimes mistakenly called – cause thousands of deaths worldwide every year. Trying to swim against them is futile, but they can be escaped by moving parallel to the beach. Most rip currents are no more than 10 m wide and they flow through much calmer water.

Wave erosion

Where waves pound against cliffs and headlands, the energy they release can produce rapid erosion, dramatically pushing back the coastline over a number of years. For example, along the 60 km long Holderness coast of East Yorkshire, cliffs are being eroded at a rate of about 2 m a year. This wave erosion occurs in two main ways. First, as waves hurl beach material – sand and pebbles – against cliffs, they wear away at the rock. Second, the wave action compresses air within tiny cracks and cavities in the rocks. As the air re-expands, it can explosively shatter the rock.

Where a coast contains headlands, wave energy tends to be concentrated on these through the effects of wave refraction. As waves wear away at a headland, various coastal features tend to develop in a classic sequence. Typically, caves first develop at the base of cliffs on either side of the headland, usually along planes of weakness in the rock. Wave action gradually widens and deepens the caves until they penetrate through the headland and an arch forms. Finally, the roof of the arch collapses to leave an isolated rock pillar called a stack, which is ultimately eroded down to a stump. Famous examples of stacks include the Twelve Apostles off the south-west coast of Victoria, Australia, and the Old Man of Hoy in the Orkney islands off northern Scotland.

SURFING

THERE IS ONE GROUP OF PEOPLE TO WHOM
WAVES ARE SO IMPORTANT THEY BECOME A WAY
OF LIFE – SURFERS. When they are not on the ocean
surfing, surfers are talking about it or anticipating the next
big swell. The sport originated in Hawaii some time before the
15th century, but it has diversified hugely over the years.
The aim of modern-day surfers is not just to attain full control
over their boards and avoid a 'wipe-out' (falling off), but also to
execute skilled manoeuvres, such as the 'floater' (riding the
breaking crest of a wave), the 'cutback' (turning towards the
wave crest) and the holy grail of surfing, 'tuberiding' – surfing
inside the barrel formed by a large breaking wave.

**'When surfing Waimea it is essential
to have the proper crazed attitude
that implies a certain reckless
disregard for personal safety. ...
If you begin to wonder what in the
world you're doing out among those
menacing waves, it's time to be
thankful you're still alive and head
for the beach.'**

From *Surfer's Guide to Hawaii*,
by Greg Ambrose

What makes good waves

Many variables are involved in creating good surfing waves,
which is why they occur only in certain places. The most
important is the structure of the seafloor leading up to the
beach. This has to have a shallow enough slope for waves to
break a little way offshore, so that they can be ridden in. Its
composition is also important. Sand produces slow-moving,
'mushy' breakers, which are fine for beginners, but it takes
rocky shores or reefs to generate the classic fast-moving barrel
waves most closely associated with surfing.

Another factor is the shape and
orientation of the coast relative to
prevailing winds. Headlands that face
directly into prevailing winds constitute
'point breaks'. For a stretch on either
side, the waves run almost parallel to the
coast, which means they can be ridden for
relatively long distances. More common
are beaches that face into the wind. Here

**'Knowing the sport
is deadly and still
choosing to do it
shows our love
for it.'**

Dave Kalama,
professional surfer

the waves break close to shore and can only be ridden short
distances, although reefs beneath the surface farther out may
cause them to break earlier.

A sport for chiefs

In Hawaii, surfing – called *he'e nalu* ('wave-sliding') – had religious
significance and was associated with power. Only chieftains and
people of high rank were allowed to surf on certain beaches,
while *kahunas* (priests) prayed and chanted to coax large waves
from the sea. Its worldwide popularity exploded from the
1950s, as cheaper glass fibre and foam boards
came onto the market, while cult movies, such as
Bruce Brown's documentary *The Endless Summer*
(1966), helped to spread its appeal. Today, it is a
pastime for tens of thousands. Some use jet skis
to tow them out to waves that were previously
impossible to reach. Others windsurf on boards
equipped with sails, or they kitesurf, using parachute-
shaped kites to pull them up and over waves.

THE PERFECT WAVE

Southern California; Oahu, Hawaii; Teahupoo, Tahiti; Saqurema, Brazil; Pico Alto and Chicama, Peru; Byron Bay, Kirra and Burleigh Heads, Australia; Piha and Manu Bay, New Zealand; Green Point and Jeffrey's Bay, South Africa; Hikkaduwa, Sri Lanka; Grajagan, Java; Uluwatu, Bali; Aurora, Philippines

EVERY SURFER DREAMS OF THE PERFECT WAVE, AND FOR EXPERT SURFERS THIS WILL UNQUESTIONABLY BE A MONSTER THAT FORMS A HUGE GLASSY-LOOKING HOLLOW TUBE OR 'BARREL' AS IT BREAKS. For 'tuberiding', it is also important that the wave does not break at many points along its length simultaneously – instead the break must progress smoothly in one direction, either to the right (a 'right-breaker', as above) or to the left (a 'left-breaker'). These waves are a trademark of legendary surf beaches, such as Waimea Bay and the Banzai Pipeline on Oahu, Hawaii.

The perfect wave will rear at least 6 m high when it breaks. Waves of this size generally occur only on shores that face onto extensive fetches (stretches of ocean), where wave-generating winds have been blowing with considerable strength for many hours. The north shore of Oahu is a classic example: it is adjacent to a fetch that is thousands of kilometres long and subject to frequent storms. To produce a wave crest that breaks to right or left, the slope of the seabed should be slightly off the right angle in relation to the direction of wave motion. Under these conditions, the wave breaks at the shallowest point initially and then progressively along the crest as it moves onshore.

During the surfing season at the Banzai Pipeline, the massive barrel-forming waves rear up and start breaking around 90 m offshore over a shallow lava rock reef. At that point they are closing in on the beach at about 8 m per second. Once the barrel forms, it progresses to the left along the wave front at about 10 m per second. Riding the Pipeline gives a short but adrenaline-pumping experience lasting 15 seconds or so, during which the surfer may travel a few hundred metres, partly towards but mostly parallel to the shoreline. At other places, such as Jeffrey's Bay in South Africa, it is sometimes possible to ride a single wave for over 1 km, on a trip lasting more than 2 minutes.

TSUNAMIS REPRESENT THE POWER OF THE OCEAN AT ITS MOST TERRIFYING. Most often triggered by a cataclysmic underwater earthquake, a tsunami is a series of waves that can travel the entire length of an ocean at the speed of a jet airliner. These waves generally pass unnoticed across the open ocean but deliver colossal destructive energy when they reach land. Large, headline-dominating tsunamis are rare events, occurring once or twice a decade at most, and the chances of any particular spot in the world being hit in a lifetime are small. But the rarity of tsunamis also increases their danger, because people tend to settle and build on coastlines that are vulnerable to them without consideration of the potential for disaster. Although some parts of the world are more likely than others to experience a big tsunami in future, no low-lying coastal area is entirely without risk.

What causes tsunamis?

Tsunamis are sometimes referred to as tidal waves, which is misleading as they have nothing to do with tides. Unlike normal surface waves, they are also not caused by the wind. Even the word 'tsunami', which translated literally from Japanese means 'harbour wave', is something of a misnomer.

Geologists call tsunamis 'seismic sea waves', and this is the best description, because most of them are caused by seismic events – in other words, earthquakes – on the ocean floor. These earthquakes result from sudden, large-scale shifts in the positions of neighbouring tectonic plates, the massive pieces of crust that make up Earth's surface layer. Other, less common causes of tsunamis are large-scale slumping of material down slopes on the seafloor; gigantic landslides from islands or mainland coasts into the ocean; submarine volcanic eruptions; or the impact of asteroids or comets from outer space. All of these events cause a sudden, massive displacement of a huge volume of ocean water, and this displacement sets off the tsunami waves.

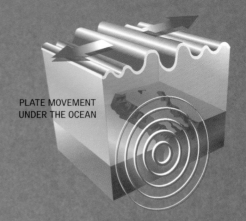

PLATE MOVEMENT UNDER THE OCEAN

MASSIVE IMPACT Most tsunamis are caused by submarine earthquakes resulting in plate movement on the ocean floor (above). If a section of the seabed moves, the water column above moves with it. Volcanic eruptions and landslides on the seafloor cause tsunamis in much the same way (opposite, below): as material is forced into the sea or moves on the seabed, it displaces the water above it. Impacts from large asteroids are rare but have caused massive tsunamis – for example, when an asteroid crashed into the Gulf of Mexico 65 million years ago.

WAVE OF DESTRUCTION An amateur photographer caught the moment when the tsunami thundered onto a beach in southern Thailand on Boxing Day 2004. The giant waves recurred at roughly 30-minute intervals, the third and most powerful one striking southern Thailand about 11am local time.

TSUNAMI

A series of waves

A tsunami is not an individual wave, but rather a series of waves that ripple out from the source, following one another across the ocean until the source area settles down again and the waves die out.

As they surge across the open ocean, tsunami waves behave differently from ordinary ocean waves in several respects. First, their wave length (the distance between wave crests) is much greater, anything from 55 to 200 km, and they travel much faster, generally at speeds ranging from 500 to 800 km/h. Second, even in the open ocean their velocity is affected by the depth of the water, because the entire water column participates in the wave motion. As a result, the deeper the ocean, the faster they can travel. Third, the waves of a tsunami are hardly noticeable at the surface of the ocean because their height – generally only about 30-60 cm – is exceedingly small compared to their wave length, so their presence is usually masked by ocean swell. Finally, the time between successive wave crests in a tsunami is much longer than for normal waves – usually something between 10 minutes and an hour.

It is when they arrive at coasts that tsunamis fully demonstrate how different they are from ordinary waves. As a tsunami approaches the shore, and the water becomes shallower, the waves slow down, but the energy they carry forces them to build rapidly in height. Frequently, this causes an undertow that drags water from shorelines directly out to sea, creating within a few seconds an apparent 'low tide' – a telltale sign of impending destruction.

An unstoppable tide

By the time a tsunami wave reaches the shore it may have grown into a towering mass of water up to 30 m high. But as it encounters land, the effect is not usually that of a mountainous wave crashing down – the wave may not even break as it hits the shore. Eyewitness accounts and video records more often give the impression of an extremely powerful onrushing tide, which flows relentlessly for several minutes and forces its way through or around anything it encounters. Most damage is caused by the enormous mass of water behind the initial wave front. Large objects, such as trees, ships ripped from their moorings and boulders, can be carried several miles inland. Buildings are sometimes obliterated to their foundations, and exposed ground is scoured down to the underlying bedrock.

The impact that a tsunami has on land is strongly affected by the shape of the coastline and the angle at which the waves hit. Shores directly facing the source of the tsunami are most at risk. Bays, harbours and river mouths also amplify the waves, and often see the worst devastation. Headlands, on the other hand, deflect them.

The first in a series of tsunami waves is not necessarily the worst or most destructive. The first wave is often followed, at intervals ranging from a few minutes up to an hour or so, by several additional waves that can compound the damage caused by the first. After each wave, much of the water in the inundated area, and some of the debris it has left in its wake, as well as living and dead bodies, are pulled out to sea again.

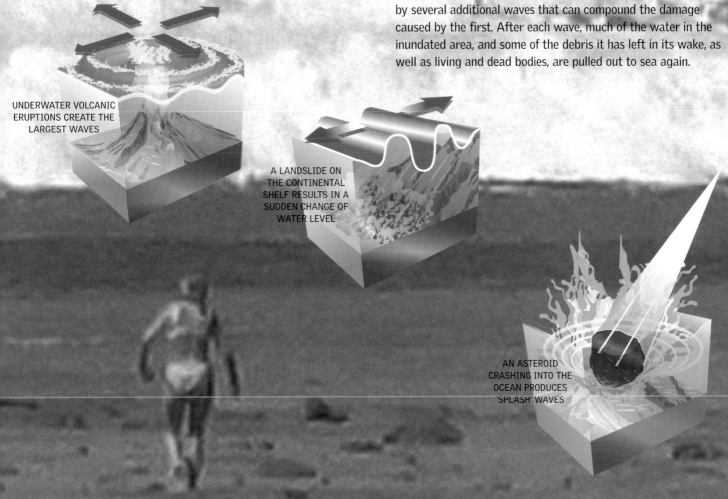

UNDERWATER VOLCANIC ERUPTIONS CREATE THE LARGEST WAVES

A LANDSLIDE ON THE CONTINENTAL SHELF RESULTS IN A SUDDEN CHANGE OF WATER LEVEL

AN ASTEROID CRASHING INTO THE OCEAN PRODUCES 'SPLASH' WAVES

A tsunami recorded in Hawaii on April 1, 1946, is typical. The course of the waves, which originated from an earthquake in the Aleutian Trench, off the Alaskan island of Unimak, was well documented from beginning to end. In the open ocean, they had a height of 30cm and a wavelength of 150km. Travelling at 760km/h they took less than 5 hours to reach the main island of Hawaii. Although they had gone virtually unnoticed by shipping at sea, when they hit the coast they were 17m high. One after another, they battered the island, each separated from the next by a 12-minute gap. The destruction they caused on the north side of Hawaii was almost total. In the coastal town of Hilo, every house on the main street was washed away. In total, the tsunami killed 165 people in Hawaii and Alaska.

Warning systems

The Hawaiian tsunami of 1946 led to the development of the Pacific Tsunami Warning Center, based in Hawaii, which later became the headquarters of the International Pacific Tsunami Warning System. This works partly by detecting earthquakes in the Pacific region that are large enough to trigger tsunamis and partly by the early detection of tsunamis themselves through a network of gauges that monitor sea level for any abnormal changes. If the system detects a tsunami, or if it measures an earthquake that meets known criteria for generating a tsunami, a warning is issued to coastal areas in the predicted path of the waves, with estimated arrival times.

While they cannot predict exactly when tsunamis will happen, scientists have been able to identify many of the areas of highest risk around the Pacific. Among the areas likely to be affected in future are the coasts of Central America, California, western Canada, the Solomon Islands, Papua New Guinea and north-western Australia. As with the earthquakes that will trigger these events, the question is not if they will happen, but when.

SCREEN TEST Computer simulations of tsunamis help scientists to identify areas of coast most at risk. Predicting when tsunamis will occur remains beyond our abilities.

NOTABLE TSUNAMIS

Most large tsunamis in the past have occurred around the edges of the Pacific Ocean. The reason for this is that the Pacific Rim contains many tectonic plate boundaries where oceanic crust is being forced underneath the crust of a neighbouring plate. This causes underwater earthquakes – each small yellow dot on the map above represents a known earthquake. The same type of plate boundary occurs in the Indian Ocean, and it was this that shifted in the December 2004 earthquake off Sumatra. Nevertheless, Pacific Ocean tsunamis are far more common. The dates beside large dots on the map indicate famously destructive tsunamis, also described below.

1700 On January 26, an earthquake off Vancouver, Canada, created a tsunami that was recorded in Japan and remembered in the oral traditions of local native North American tribes.
1883 On August 26, the explosion of the volcano Krakatoa in Indonesia caused tsunami waves in the Indian and Pacific Oceans. Waves 40 m high were logged on some coasts.
1960 On May 22, the greatest earthquake ever recorded, off Chile, caused a tsunami that ran through the Pacific Ocean and devastated Hawaii, as well as coastal regions of South America.
1993 On July 12, a tsunami occurred as a result of an earthquake off the island of Hokkaido, Japan. Waves up to 31 m high were recorded, and there were 239 fatalities.
1998 On July 17, a tsunami of 15 m high waves hit Papua New Guinea, causing over 2200 deaths.

SUMATRA – DECEMBER 26, 2004

DECEMBER 26, 2004, BROUGHT THE DEADLIEST TSUNAMI IN RECORDED HISTORY. It swamped the coastlines of 12 countries and claimed at least 150 000 human lives, and possibly as many as 275 000. The earthquake that caused the tsunami occurred at 7.59 am local time just north of Simeulue Island, off the north-west coast of Sumatra. Measuring over 9 on the Richter Scale, it was the largest earthquake recorded anywhere in the world for more than 40 years. Its magnitude was such that the planet itself wobbled on its axis.

Tremors shook the Earth's crust as a section of the India Plate slipped 15 m under the neighbouring Eurasian Plate, in a north-eastern area of the Indian Ocean. As this happened, a rupture in the Earth's crust occurred some 30 km below the seabed and spread along the boundary between the two plates, in two stages. Beginning near Aceh in northern Sumatra, the rupture ran in a north-westerly direction, taking just under 2 minutes to reach a length of around 400 km. It then paused for about 100 seconds before continuing northwards, more slowly, to an area close to the Andaman and Nicobar Islands, extending its total length to some 1200 km. As the tectonic plate sections

slipped past each other, the seabed along the entire length of the rupture was raised several metres, displacing a huge quantity of seawater – an estimated 30 km³ – and setting off the tsunami.

The spread of the disaster

The tsunami spread out from the entire length of this vast area of seabed disturbance. The first large area of land to be hit was Aceh in Sumatra. The Andaman and Nicobar Islands were struck almost simultaneously, but it was another hour before the waves made landfall in Myanmar (Burma). They hit Sri Lanka, the east coast of mainland India and Thailand around 90 minutes to 2 hours after the earthquake, and the Maldives three and a half hours after it. The tsunami took 7 hours to cross the Indian Ocean and reach Somalia and 12 hours to reach South Africa, where its most distant fatality was recorded.

The height of the waves on impact varied greatly. Along the coast of Aceh they reached 24 m at the coast and rose to 30 m high as they thundered inland. Elsewhere, they were smaller but still devastating, inundating areas up to 2 km from the shore. The most powerful waves ran east and west of the earthquake zone because of the almost north-south orientation of the fault line. As a result, Sri Lanka suffered terrible casualties, while Bangladesh, at roughly the same distance from the source area, was much less affected.

EARTH SHAKER The Boxing Day earthquake released energy equivalent to 100 gigatons of TNT – about as much energy as the USA uses in six months. Unlike most earthquakes, which last a few seconds, this one continued for nearly 10 minutes. The landmasses of Sumatra and the Malay Peninsula blocked the progress of the tsunami, so places beyond them were spared the devastation.

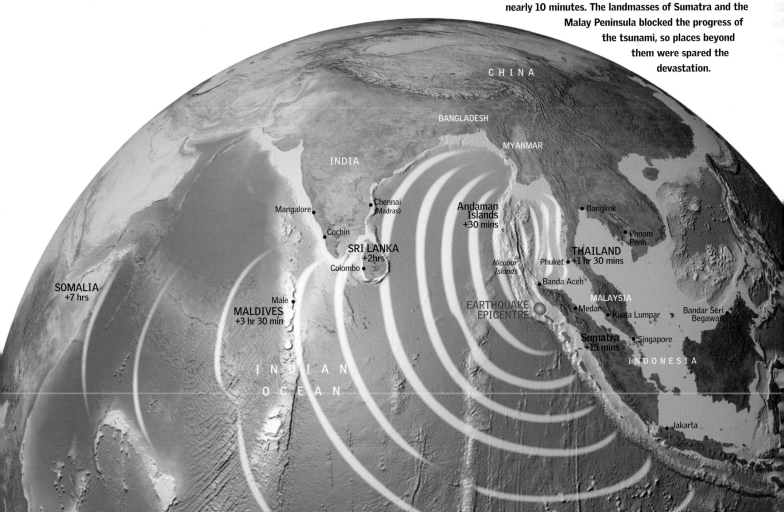

AFTER THE WAVES

AFTER THE INDIAN OCEAN TSUNAMI, STATES OF EMERGENCY WERE DECLARED IN INDONESIA, SRI LANKA AND THE MALDIVES. This prompted a huge worldwide effort to help victims, with a total of over US$3 billion offered by governments and individuals. Relief agencies initially warned of the possibility of more deaths to come as a result of epidemics caused by poor sanitation. Thanks to the relief efforts, however, by February 2005 such epidemics seemed to have been largely averted.

As well as the heavy toll on human life, the tsunami has had a major environmental impact that is likely to affect many coastal regions of the Indian Ocean for several years to come. It inflicted severe damage on coastal ecosystems, such as coral reefs, coastal wetlands and mangrove forests. In addition, in some regions heavy saltwater infiltration poisoned wells and aquifers used to supply fresh water.

Unlike the Pacific, the Indian Ocean had no tsunami early warning system. Within a few weeks of the 2004 tsunami, a United Nations conference held in Kobe, Japan, decided that a warning system should be established as soon as possible. In September 2005, the government of India announced that it was intending to fund the setting up of an initial warning system to be in operation by the year 2007.

'I struggled through the water, joining the crowds running for higher ground, some carrying their dead and injured. White-capped floodwaters raced over the streets and between houses. Bodies of children were entangled in wire mesh used to barricade seaside homes. Bodies were carried up to the road, covered with sarongs and laid out for relatives to find. Rows and rows of women and men stood on the road, asking if anyone has seen their loved ones.'

**Amarasinghe, survivor,
Sri Lanka**

LOST CITY *Before the tsunami, Banda Aceh on Sumatra was a thriving city. The immense waves swept away almost everything, leaving only the sturdiest buildings, such as the central mosque, standing.*

'If you go to Aceh today, you see vast areas ... where it's like a nuclear explosion has taken place. Not even any rubble is left. The force of the water was so great that not only did it destroy houses, but it took all of the rubble out to sea. It's the most eerie, tragic, surreal sight.'

Andrew Steer, World Bank
Country Director for Indonesia

FLOODED LANDSCAPE *The tsunami rushed far inland, inundating huge areas with seawater. Here, vehicles pick their way along the raised coastal road near Batticaloa in eastern Sri Lanka.*

'I heard a huge roar and when I looked back there was a massive wave rushing down the lane behind us, wiping out everything it touched ... A woman holding a baby asked me what was going on and all I could say was: "The water's coming". The next second we were all under water being tossed around, as if we were in a huge washing machine full of rubble.'

Felix, survivor,
Koh Phi Phi, Thailand

LIFE AT THE
EDGE

4

THE SHALLOW WATERS AROUND THE COASTS ARE SOME OF THE MOST PRODUCTIVE IN THE OCEAN. The close proximity of seabed, sea surface and land creates a combination of habitats that supports a huge variety of life. Most of the world's coral reefs, for example, are in coastal waters – home to creatures such as this black-tipped reef shark. The power of the tides is most noticeable around the coasts, as every day the planet's liquid surface is dragged back and forth. This ebb and flow of the tides, which occurs twice daily in most parts of the oceans, is an eternal cycle, so integral to the life of our planet that most of us take it for granted. The invisible forces that drive this constant, inexorable motion stem from the Earth's gravitational interaction with the Sun and, above all, the Moon.

TIDES

ALTHOUGH PREDICTABLE, TIDES VARY ALL OVER THE WORLD. Complex factors – from the speed at which waves pass through the ocean to the shape and position of landmasses – contribute to variations in tidal strength, size, speed and even the number of tides each day. The general principles of how tides work are straightforward, however, following patterns dictated by the positions of the Moon and Sun relative to the Earth. These patterns follow two cycles: one daily, the other monthly.

THE SILVER ORB A Full Moon rising over the Sea of Cortez off Mexico's Baja California coast. At the time of both Full Moon and New Moon, gravitational interaction with the Sun reinforces the normal tidal bulges associated with the Moon to produce strong 'spring' tides.

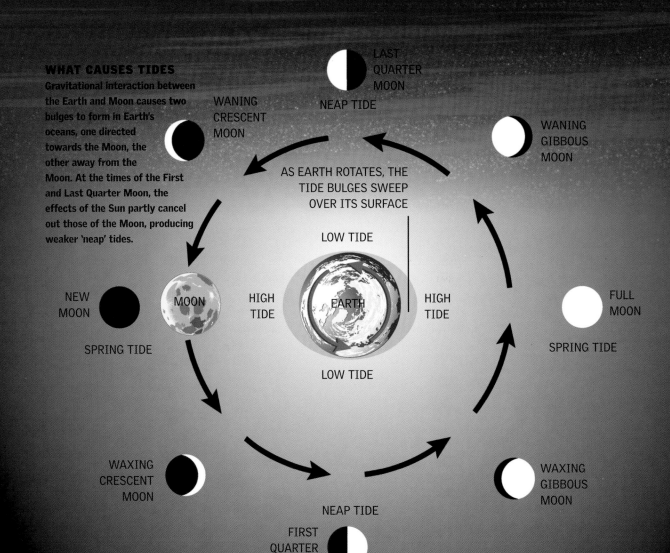

WHAT CAUSES TIDES

Gravitational interaction between the Earth and Moon causes two bulges to form in Earth's oceans, one directed towards the Moon, the other away from the Moon. At the times of the First and Last Quarter Moon, the effects of the Sun partly cancel out those of the Moon, producing weaker 'neap' tides.

LAST QUARTER MOON
NEAP TIDE

WANING CRESCENT MOON

WANING GIBBOUS MOON

AS EARTH ROTATES, THE TIDE BULGES SWEEP OVER ITS SURFACE

LOW TIDE

SUN

NEW MOON
SPRING TIDE

MOON

HIGH TIDE

EARTH

HIGH TIDE

FULL MOON
SPRING TIDE

LOW TIDE

WAXING CRESCENT MOON

NEAP TIDE

FIRST QUARTER MOON

WAXING GIBBOUS MOON

THE WORLD'S BIGGEST TIDES

The difference in sea level between high and low tide varies enormously across the world, from close to zero to tens of metres. Listed below are the world's largest tidal ranges, by country – Canada and Britain both have several points with tidal ranges higher than anywhere else. All of the ranges listed peak during the fortnightly spring tides.

COUNTRY	LOCATION	MAXIMUM RANGE	AVERAGE RANGE
Canada	Burntcoat Head, Bay of Fundy, Nova Scotia	17.0 m	11.9 m
Britain	Avonmouth, Bristol Channel	15.5 m	9.7 m
France	Granville	14.7 m	8.7 m
Russia	Cape Astronomicheski, Kamchatka	13.9 m	7.4 m
USA (Alaska)	Sunrise, Turnagain Arm, Cook Inlet	12.7 m	9.4 m
Argentina	Río Gallegos (Reducción Beacon)	11.9 m	8.9 m
Australia	Shale Island, Collier Bay	11.6 m	unknown
Denmark (Greenland)	Koksoak River entrance, Hudson Bay	10.7 m	8.8 m
Chile	Banco Dirección, Magellan Strait	unknown	8.6 m

High tide, low tide – the daily cycle

The daily cycle results chiefly from two opposing forces caused by the gravitational interplay between the Earth and Moon. One of these pulls things towards the Moon, the other pulls away from it, and both are exerted at every point on Earth.

The first force is gravitational – the pull of the Moon's gravity, which acts most strongly on the parts of the Earth nearest to it. The second is centrifugal, a force directed away from an axis of rotation and seen if you whirl an object on a string around your head – if the string breaks, the object is flung farther away. The centrifugal force involved in causing tides results from a little-known aspect of the Earth-Moon system. Although the Moon is usually thought of as orbiting Earth's centre, in fact both bodies orbit around their common centre of mass, which is a point located inside the Earth but not at its centre. This means that as the Moon orbits the Earth, our planet executes a little movement of its own around the centre of mass, and this produces the centrifugal force. It is always directed away from the Moon and is the same everywhere on Earth.

Over the Earth as a whole the two forces balance, but at specific points within the oceans, imbalances exist. The gravitational force is slightly greater on the side of the Earth facing the Moon, causing ocean water on that side to be drawn towards the Moon. The centrifugal force predominates on the side facing away, causing water there to be pushed away from the Moon. If the Earth were uniformly covered with water, there would be two 'bulges' in its ocean surface, one pointing towards the Moon, the other, on the opposite side, away from it – hence, the twice-daily rise and fall of tides at most points in the oceans. As the Earth spins on its axis, the tidal bulges 'sweep' over its surface, and in a planet uniformly covered with water, each point would experience two rises in sea level every day as the bulges pass over, followed by a drop in level as they move on.

In reality, of course, the Earth is not uniformly covered with water. The presence of landmasses and ocean basins of variable depth means that the actual pattern of daily tides is far more complex. There is, however, one universally constant characteristic of the daily tidal pattern: the regular way in which the timings of high and low tides shift forwards by about 50 minutes a day. The reason for this is quite simple. Each day, the Moon moves forwards a little in its orbit around the Earth, so as the Earth spins, an additional 50 minutes is necessary for a spot on its surface to regain its position relative to the Moon – a 'lunar day' therefore lasts 24 hours and 50 minutes.

Springs and neaps – the monthly cycle

The monthly cycle of the tides is driven by Earth's gravitational interaction with the Sun in combination with the effect of the Moon. Despite its vastly greater size, the Sun's tide-producing effect on the Earth's oceans is less than half that of the Moon because it is so much farther away. Nevertheless, the Earth's orbit round the Sun produces forces that tend to cause bulges in its oceans both towards and away from the Sun.

Twice a month, the Sun, Moon and Earth are aligned – at the New Moon, when the Moon lies between the Earth and the Sun, and two weeks later at the Full Moon, when the Moon lies directly opposite the Sun on the far side of the Earth. Around these times, the tidal bulges produced by the Sun tend to reinforce those produced by the Moon, and so overall there are much larger bulges than usual. As a consequence, the high tides tend to be exceptionally high at these times of the month (and for a day or two afterwards), while the low tides are exceptionally low. These tides are called spring tides – not after the season, but from 'spring' in the sense of 'to rise up' or 'to leap'.

By contrast, at the times of the First and Last Quarter Moons, which occur a week after the New and Full Moons, the Sun lies at right angles to the direction of the Moon. At these times, the tide-producing effects of the two bodies cancel each other out to some extent, and this brings tides with the smallest range (the least difference between high and low water) in the monthly cycle. They are called neap tides, from an Old English word meaning 'low' or 'to nip'.

IN AND OUT Land is exposed and covered as the tides ebb and rise again. Where the slope of the shore is shallow, as here along Scotland's Firth of Forth, large expanses of beach appear at low tide, then disappear hours later.

TIDAL RANGE

AS LONG AS THE WORLD KEEPS TURNING, TIDES WILL EBB AND FLOW, BUT THEY DO NOT RISE AND FALL EVENLY IN ALL PARTS OF THE WORLD. On the contrary, the variety in tidal range – the difference in sea level between high and low water – is immense. Among the many factors determining these variations, the most important is the shape of the coastline. For example, bays act like funnels, amplifying the water's rise. Tides also reach higher where they are forced through narrow straits or into estuaries and river mouths. And they are affected by water depth. Out in the open ocean, the tidal range is generally small, averaging about 60 cm, but along the world's coasts, where the water is shallower, it can be many times greater: in some places over 10 m. Coasts reflect tides, too – that is, tides bounce off them, affecting the height of tides elsewhere.

High rise

The Bay of Fundy on Canada's Atlantic coast has the world's greatest tidal range, reaching its peak in the Minas Basin at the extreme eastern end of the bay. Here, the average range is 11.9 m, and during the highest spring tides this increases to 17 m – higher than a four-storey building.

The shape of the bay and its dimensions are key factors. Every large body of water has its own natural rocking motion from one end to the other and back again – a type of wave called a 'seiche'. In the Bay of Fundy, this natural rhythm repeats roughly every 13 hours, which almost coincides with the tidal cycle (the time between one high tide and the next) of 12 hours and 25 minutes – half a lunar day (see page 65). As the tide rises, ocean water flooding in from the Gulf of Maine amplifies the existing motion of the water in the bay, making it oscillate higher and higher – somewhat like water being sloshed from end to end of a bathtub. In addition, the bay becomes narrower and shallower in its upper reaches, pushing the water still higher up its shores. The volume of water forced into the bay at each tide is so great, it actually causes the Earth's crust in that area to dip. The surrounding Nova Scotia countryside tilts very slightly as the tide comes in, then bounces back as it goes out.

The world's second highest tidal range is in the Bristol Channel, which divides south-western England from Wales. Here, waters may rise and fall by over 15 m in the space of just a few hours. It is the shape of the coast the causes this enormous range. The Bristol Channel joins the estuary of the River Severn, and together the two form a gigantic funnel, 45 km wide at its mouth but narrowing to less than 10 km by the time it reaches Clevedon, near Bristol. As the tide rises, the huge volume of water that enters at the estuary's wide mouth is forced farther and farther up the shore in the narrower and shallower parts of the funnel.

Another phenomenon associated with high tidal ranges is a tidal bore. As the tide rushes into a river, it sometimes creates a wall of water, called a bore, along its front. The bore on the River Severn occasionally reaches heights of 2.8 m and is sometimes still visible as far north as Gloucester. The world's largest bore forms in Hangzhou Bay, south of Shanghai, which also has an extremely large tidal range, as the bay narrows and quickly becomes shallow. During the highest tides, the bore in Hangzhou Bay can reach heights of 7.5 m and be heard approaching 22 km away.

Low or no rise

In contrast, some areas of water in the middle of oceans have scarcely any tidal range at all. The reason for this concerns the way that tides are generated.

The underlying cause of tides is the Earth's interaction with the Moon and Sun that creates 'bulges' of water, which sweep over the ocean surface as the planet spins (see pages 64-65). In practice, the presence of large landmasses prevents these bulges from moving around the planet in an unrestricted fashion. What is actually created are bulges of water that swirl in a rotary motion, every 12 hours and 25 minutes, around large, roughly circular areas of ocean – for example, around the North Atlantic.

In essence, the bulges are massively energetic waves, with very long wave lengths. The regions containing them are called amphidromic systems. There are separate amphidromic systems for the effects of the Moon and the Sun – although the lunar one is more important – and these combine to produce the tidal patterns that we experience. At the centre of each system – rather like the eye at the centre of a hurricane – is an amphidromic point, where there is hardly any tidally generated movement of water at all.

Most amphidromic points occur in the open ocean, but there is one caused by the Moon's amphidromic system in the Pacific that falls very close to the islands of Tahiti. As a result,

BOARDING THE BORE A Brazilian surfer rides the pororoca *tidal bore on a tributary of the Amazon. The* pororoca, *from a native Indian word meaning 'big roar', can travel at over 30 km/h and reach more than 300 km inland.*

Tahiti's tides are highly unusual. With hardly any lunar-created tide, the twice daily tidal rise and fall is driven instead entirely by the Sun, with high tides occurring at around midday and midnight, and its low tides near sunrise and sunset. The total range of the tide is barely 30 cm. While the Sun's gravity affects the height of tides elsewhere in the world, its impact is so small compared with that of the Moon that in most places its effect is barely noticed.

Other parts of the world with very small tidal ranges include seas cut off from the main oceans. The average range in the Mediterranean and Black Sea, for example, is less than 1 m, due to the narrowness of their connection to the Atlantic.

Variable tides

The most common daily pattern of tides worldwide consists of two high tides, of near equal height, and two low tides. These are called semidiurnal tides. Some areas, such as parts of the Gulf of Mexico, experience just one high tide and one low tide a day (called diurnal tides), but most regions without semidiurnal tides have so-called 'mixed' tides. In these, the range between high and low waters each day is variable. One of the high tides or one of the low tides (or both) has a very different height from the other. Many coastal areas, including many Pacific coasts, experience mixed tides.

An unusual feature of Southampton on the south coast of England – and one of the reasons for its success as a port – is that it has four high tides and two low tides a day. Pairs of closely grouped high tides occur every 12 hours or so, split by single low tides. The Isle of Wight, lying between Southampton and the English Channel, explains this phenomenon. As a tidal pulse, or bulge, originating in the Atlantic moves up the English Channel, it initially reaches Southampton via the western Solent, the body of water north-west of the Isle of Wight, to produce the first tidal peak. Simultaneously, the pulse moves round the south of the Isle of Wight, then up its eastern coast into the eastern Solent to produce a second tidal peak in Southampton. This is one example of how even small islands, not just larger landmasses, can affect the flow of the tides.

Harnessing tidal power

The energy held in tides is immense. Twice a day, the tides lift 14 billion tonnes of water over 10 m in the Bay of Fundy alone. The energy expended each time this happens is close to 1.5 million megawatts, or more than four times the combined capacity of all the world's nuclear power stations. Harnessing tidal power offers potentially enormous rewards. It has been estimated, for example, that tidal power could supply 20 per cent of

EXTREME TIDE

THE ENORMOUS ENERGY

OF THE TIDES IN EARTH'S OCEANS IS USUALLY HIDDEN, SPREAD THROUGH WATER THAT RISES AND FALLS IMPERCEPTIBLY. In places, however, the true strength of a tide becomes visible as it forces seawater through narrow gaps between bodies of land. The fierce currents that form in these channels can flow faster than most small boats, making them treacherous places to sail. The world's most extreme tidal current forms about 30 km east of the Norwegian city of Bodø. Known as the Saltstraumen, it reaches speeds of up to 40 km/h (22 knots) as it roars through a 3 km-long, 150 m-wide strait between two headlands. The churning waters spin off vortices 10 m across that can pull objects down beneath the waves.

The reason for this extreme tidal current is that the strait forms a bottleneck between two bodies of water. Inland is the Skjerstad fjord, and the Saltstraumen forms as the tide strains to fill the fjord. The bottleneck forces the seawater outside to rise faster than the water inside. As the two levels diverge, the current becomes ever stronger as the tide pours in. The Saltstraumen forms four times a day, with the tide flowing out just as fiercely as it flows in. Because the current is tidal, it is most powerful just after the Full and New Moons – during periods of spring tides. Local folklore has it that the Saltstraumen is at its most violent every year on Good Friday. This myth is close to the truth, as Good Friday always falls near a spring tide – Easter is the Sunday following the first Full Moon after March 20.

Britain's energy needs using technology that is already available. It may seem surprising, therefore, that relatively few tidal power plants are currently in operation, but this is explained partly by the expense involved in building them, and partly by the effect they have on the local environment.

Most existing plants work rather like hydroelectric dams. Giant sluice gates are opened to allow water to flow into a bay or estuary as the tide rises, then closed at high tide to hold it there. Once the tide has fallen sufficiently on the seaward side of the dam, the water is gradually released through hydroelectric turbines and flows back into the sea. The supply of fuel is free and endless, but the drawback is that such stations can damage the ecosystems of the bays and estuaries where they are located. Planning and building tidal power stations requires careful consideration, weighing up the benefits of pollution-free electricity generation against the potential environmental impact.

Another limiting factor is the local tidal range. Where the total rise and fall is less than 5 m, tidal power plants are inefficient, and the cost of running and maintaining them will outweigh the profit that can be generated from the electricity produced. Most coasts have only a few sites where conditions are right for building one.

HARNESSING NATURE The world's largest tidal power station spans the River Rance near St-Malo in Brittany. Completed in 1966, it makes a significant contribution to Brittany's electricity supply.

While coastal dam power stations are controversial, other systems have been developed that are less damaging environmentally. Most have the advantage of being positioned offshore where they can operate without having a major impact on wildlife. For example, turbine stations have been designed that work rather like wind farms under the sea. Large rotor blades are driven by the inward flow of water and their rotation is used to generate electricity. The first commercial-scale offshore turbine tidal power station was completed in 2003 off Lynmouth in south-west England. While it has not yet been connected to the national grid (for cost reasons), it has been fully tested and shown to work efficiently. The company behind it is now in the process of designing and building the world's first grid-connected offshore turbine tidal power station, due to go into operation in 2007.

Other groups, such as the Canadian company Blue Energy, are also developing offshore turbine systems that could make use of both the inward and outward flow of the tides. Blue Energy's design is based on a traditional water mill, but with a vertical (rather than the usual horizontal) axis, which would be fixed to the seabed in areas with strong tidal currents. Although still at the testing stage, it has the potential to be extended to form gigantic submarine 'fences' several kilometres long, generating electricity all along their length. Should these ever be built, each could generate thousands of megawatts of power and be a serious alternative to both fossil fuel and nuclear power stations.

RACES AND WHIRLPOOLS

THE RISE AND FALL OF THE TIDES NEAR COASTS CAN PRODUCE POWERFUL, FAST-FLOWING MOVEMENTS OF WATER, called tidal races, or rapids. These surge along shores as they pour over underwater reefs or through gaps between islands or between the coast and offshore rocks. Tidal races are both powerful and unpredictable, suddenly changing direction as they flow past spurs of rock beneath the surface. In some places, these hidden obstacles cause the water to spin, generating eddies and whirlpools that can pull floating objects under. Tidal races are well known to experienced mariners and coastguards, and many have a history of wrecking vessels by dragging them onto rocks.

The Skookumchuk and St Catherine's Race

One of the most famous tidal rapids is in the Skookumchuk Narrows on British Columbia's Sunshine Coast, not far from Vancouver. Twice a day, a strong tidal flow rushes through a 300 m wide channel in the coast, pouring over a bedrock outcrop. Some 350 billion litres of seawater rush through the gap, accompanied by considerable turbulence and standing waves, to produce a 3 m rise between low and high tide. At peak, the flow rate is approximately 18 million litres per second, and current velocities of 30 km/h (16 knots) have been recorded, making the location a favourite, if dangerous, haunt for extreme kayakers.

Another notorious race forms along the shores of the Isle of Wight. Called St Catherine's Race, it happens as the tide flowing up the English Channel rushes through a gap between the south of the island and a shallow parallel ridge of offshore rock. The gap itself is known as St Catherine's Deep and the continual force of the tides has scoured out huge chasms in its bed. Over the centuries, St Catherine's Race has claimed hundreds of ships, their decks swamped by waters erupting from the Deep.

Whirlpools and boils

Many tidal races are associated with whirlpools – swirling vortices of water created by turbulence in narrow or shallow straits. Whirlpools most often occur when fast-flowing tidal streams encounter underwater obstructions such as rocks, ridges, shelves and submarine peaks. In the vortex of a whirlpool, the flow is a spiralling downward motion. A return of water to the surface occurs in the form of a rising current called a 'boil', which is visible at the surface as a heaving disturbance.

An example in the British Isles is Scotland's Corryvreckan whirlpool – Coirebhreacain in Gaelic, which means 'the cauldron of the speckled seas'. The Corryvreckan results from a tidal race that runs between the Hebridean islands of Jura and Scarba. Near its northern edge, the race forms a 400 m wide whirlpool. In 1947, the Corryvreckan almost claimed the writer George Orwell. Taking a break from writing and setting out with some young relatives for a boat ride along Jura's shores, Orwell and his companions became caught

in a powerful current, which dragged them into the whirlpool. Fortunately, his nephew managed to row the boat away from the centre of the vortex and they escaped drowning.

The Maelstrom and the Garofalo

Another whirlpool, first mentioned in Viking myth, conjures up by its very name an image of violent, chaotic turbulence – the Maelstrom. Also known as the Moskstraumen, the Maelstrom forms between the islands of Moskenesøya and Mosken off north-western Norway. Four times a day, the whirlpool springs into life as the tide surges at speeds of up to 28 km/h (15 knots) over a broad submerged causeway that links the two islands. The submarine cliffs on either side of this barrier dive steeply down to great depths, and the tide sloshes over it like water from an overflowing sink. Although fearsome, the Maelstrom's powers have often been exaggerated. In his novel *20 000 Leagues under the Sea*, Jules Verne used the Maelstrom to send Captain Nemo's *Nautilus* to its end 'where so many ships have perished'. In reality, no large ship is known ever to have been sucked into the Maelstrom or any other whirlpool.

The whirlpool of Garofalo, in the Strait of Messina between Sicily and the toe of Italy, is produced by winds that flow against the direction of local tidal currents. This type of surface turbulence is sometimes referred to as 'overfalls'. Traditionally, the Garofalo has been associated with the whirlpool of Charybdis in Homer's *Odyssey* – although some scholars believe that a more likely origin for the Charybdis story can be found near Cape Skilla in north-western Greece.

The Old Sow and the Naruto

The Old Sow off Canada's eastern seaboard and the small but lively Naruto in Japan are two more whirlpools that are sufficiently large, regular and noticeable to be regarded as more-or-less permanent coastal features. The Old Sow is the largest natural whirlpool in the western hemisphere. It is created by the confluence of two strong tidal currents near Deer Island, New Brunswick. Most often, it forms a huge area of varied kinds of turbulence in the water surface, including boils, spouts and saucer-shaped gyres. Every now and then, when tides are running especially high and coincide with strong winds, it becomes a large funnel in the water that appears to suck smaller gyres, known locally as 'piglets', into itself – although it may also throw them off.

The Naruto is in a narrow channel that separates the Japanese islands of Shikoku and Awaji, and connects the Pacific Ocean to Japan's Inland Sea. Colossal amounts of water move in and out of the Inland Sea through this channel four times a day, reaching speeds of up to 20 km/h (11 knots) during spring tides, and creating a vortex up to 20 m in diameter where they encounter a submarine ridge.

TURNED BY TIDES The Naruto whirlpools of Japan form as a tidal current – the third fastest current in the world – rushes through the strait separating the islands of Shikoku and Awaji.

SURVIVAL ON THE SHORE

THE TIDAL ENVIRONMENT PRESENTS LIFE WITH A UNIQUE SET OF CHALLENGES. Organisms have to be able to survive both in seawater and out of it, as the tide rises to cover them, then falls again leaving them exposed to the air. Most creatures that live in this world between the tides evolved from marine ancestors, so they cope by trapping seawater or carrying it with them. Shellfish that live attached to the rocks, such as barnacles and mussels, close their shells as the tide falls to hold water inside. Some more mobile creatures stay underwater by following the falling tide; others remain where they are and carry on in the air. Crabs, for example, are quite at home on the sand or rocks above the water, even though they have gills. They continue to extract oxygen from seawater inside their carapaces and make their way down to the sea's edge or rock pools when they need to replenish the supply.

Fish out of water

In the tropics, there are even fish that spend time out of the sea. Like shore crabs, mudskippers have gills which they must keep wet, yet like crabs they, too, regularly leave the water. As the name suggests, mudskippers are perfectly able to move about on land, lifting their bodies up on muscular pectoral fins. They leave the water to feed – some graze algae from the sediment; others hunt small crabs and other invertebrates. Although they occasionally have to return to the water, mudskippers can spend hours out of it if the air is humid. They breathe partly through their gills, which they keep covered with trapped seawater, partly through their skin, absorbing oxygen from the air into blood vessels concentrated near the surface.

Where the tidal shore is sandy or muddy, many creatures live in the sediment itself. Ragworms, for instance, spend their lives burrowing through seashore mud as they hunt for smaller creatures to eat. They are able to survive even at low tide because the sediment itself holds water. This enables them to continue to breathe through gills even when the sea has retreated far down the shore.

Although shore sediments may look barren, in fact they support a huge abundance of life. Muddy shores, in particular, contain large quantities of dead organic matter. This feeds bacteria and other microbes, which in turn provide food for larger organisms. While relatively few animal species live within the mud, those that do exist in communities of millions, sometimes even billions, of individuals. They form a rich food source for other creatures, because although out of sight of surface predators, they are far from out of reach. Wading birds use their probing bills to get at them, each species specialising in particular prey. Those with the longest bills, such as godwits and curlews, seek the creatures that bury themselves deepest –

PINCER MOVEMENT An American oystercatcher uses its long bladelike bill to break open bivalves on the muddy shore.

FLYING VISITORS The mud flats exposed by low tides are filled with small animals, which attract huge numbers of wading birds.

lugworms and other relatively large burrowers. Redshanks, with their slightly shorter bills, feed on bivalve molluscs such as tellin, which live nearer the surface. The smallest waders of all, birds such as knots and sanderlings, eat the little crustaceans and other creatures that have the shallowest burrows, scouring the mud in huge flocks every time the tide recedes.

Life is sparser on rocky shores than muddy ones, but even these have their own specialists. Oystercatchers break open mussels and other shellfish that cling to the rocks. Turnstones flip over seaweed and other matter to expose crabs and other small creatures hidden beneath.

The most barren beaches of all are those made of pebbles or sand. Very few animals can live among pebbles as they retain hardly any organic matter. Burrows made in sand quickly collapse, so most of the animals that live here are small enough to move through the gaps between individual grains.

Scavenging for a living

As the tides ebb and flow, they deposit material on the shore, and for a few creatures this washed-up matter is all they need to live on. Sandhoppers, for example, eat the rotting seaweed that marks the strand line (high-tide mark) on many beaches. If the seaweed is disturbed, these little crustaceans spring high into the air, propelled by a powerful flick of their tails – hence their name. Slightly larger than sandhoppers are sea slaters, close relatives of the entirely land-living woodlice. These crustaceans are quick-moving, nocturnal creatures who live among rocks and large pieces of debris near the strand line. As night falls they emerge to scavenge whatever the tide has washed up.

Among larger shoreline scavengers, seagulls are the most widespread, so common that few of us give them a second glance. The reason for seagulls' success is their great adaptability. Most will eat almost anything, living or dead.

Coastal mammals

The shallow waters that lap the world's coasts have their own unique fauna. Seals and sea lions spend their lives here, resting on sandbanks and secluded beaches in between forays hunting for fish. Along parts of North America's west coast, they share their home with sea otters, well-insulated foragers that rarely come ashore. Sea otters feed mainly on sea urchins and shellfish, smashing the shells with stones to get at the flesh inside. They even sleep on the water, taking naps lying on their backs wrapped in kelp fronds to stop themselves drifting away.

Many dolphins and porpoises spend time in coastal waters, and ten species live in them exclusively, including Hector's dolphin and the vaquita, two of the world's smallest cetaceans – neither species exceeds 1.5 m in length. Hector's dolphins live around the shores of New Zealand, while the vaquita lives in the north of the Gulf of California.

Other mammals in coastal waters include the dugong and the three species of manatee – West Indian, Amazonian and West African. These large, docile creatures are sometimes collectively called sea cows and the name is apt. Like cattle, they live by grazing, mainly on eelgrass, which grows in shallow water close to the shore. The dugong inhabits warm coasts around the Indian Ocean, while manatees live in tropical and subtropical waters in the Atlantic.

Water wings

The largest coastal animals are mostly mammals, but birds are far more numerous. While waders patrol the estuaries and beaches, other species hunt fish in the waters just offshore. Cormorants and shags live almost entirely in coastal waters, diving from the surface to catch fish in their long, hooked beaks. Terns, on the other hand, plunge-dive for their prey from the air. Some larger birds also do this, among them gannets and their more tropical cousins, the boobies. Pelicans are usually associated with fresh water but one species, the brown pelican, hunts for fish almost entirely at sea. It too dives for its prey from the air, folding its wings back at the last second in order to pierce the water like a dart.

Some seabirds hunt by using their wings to 'fly' underwater. Auks such as puffins and guillemots do this, diving down as much as 30 m after their prey. The true masters of this hunting technique are the penguins, some of which inhabit coasts surprisingly far from the South Pole. The most northerly species, the Galápagos penguin, lives almost on the Equator, although the flow of ocean currents makes the waters in which it hunts far cooler than the latitude would suggest.

Rich pickings

In terms of living things, coastal waters are generally speaking the richest part of the ocean. Because the waters are shallow, storms ensure that nutrients are kept suspended in them, rather than sinking to the bottom as they do farther out to sea. Upwelling coastal currents also help by bringing organic matter up to the surface from deep water, while a third source of nutrients is the runoff, via rivers, from land. All of this feeds microscopic algae, which make up the phytoplankton that in turn feeds planktonic animals, which in their turn are eaten by larger creatures, including filter-feeding fish, such as herring and mackerel. These and other coastal fish are also harvested in huge quantities by people. Around 90 per cent of the world's fisheries are in coastal waters.

Despite this richness, coastal waters support very few marine animal groups that are not also found elsewhere in the ocean. The very nature of the sea means that it is easy for aquatic animals to move into and colonise new areas. In the many millions of years that animal life has existed in the ocean, virtually all of its non-air-breathing groups have evolved forms that can survive in the open ocean or on the deep seabed, as well as along the coasts.

PLANTS AND ALGAE

THE TIDAL ZONE IS AN ALMOST IMPOSSIBLE HABITAT FOR PLANTS THAT CANNOT TOLERATE HAVING THEIR ROOTS IN SALT WATER, but a few specialised groups have adapted to life here. The largest and most successful are the mangroves, salt-tolerant trees, which form great thickets and even forests along many tropical and subtropical coasts. They have adapted to salt water in different ways. Some get rid of excess salt through pores at the base of their leaves; others block its absorption at the roots. Mangroves play an important role in stabilising coasts, as their tangled roots bind coastal sediments together.

Most other coastal plants grow a little way back from the strand line, but eelgrasses live beneath the water, able to tolerate high levels of salt in their tissues. The meadows they form in shallow coastal waters provide food for many animals and act as nurseries for numerous invertebrates and fish.

Seaweeds of green, red and brown

The most common photosynthesising organisms in tidal waters are seaweeds. These are not plants at all but algae, a more primitive group with its own kingdom in biological classification. Seaweeds vary greatly in shape and size but all generate food by using energy from the Sun. As a result, they are only found as far down as sunlight can reach. Some seaweeds are green like plants, but others are brown and still others red. The colours reflect the different pigments used in photosynthesis. Green seaweeds use the same kind of chlorophyll as plants. Brown seaweeds use a different variety of chlorophyll, along with another pigment called fucoxanthin. Red seaweeds use the red pigment phycoerythrin and contain no chlorophyll at all.

The largest seaweeds, called kelp, can grow to well over 30 m long, forming submarine forests with unique animal communities. Smaller seaweeds, though less spectacular, are the most common around rocky coastlines. Like kelp, they cling on with tough rootlike structures called holdfasts. Many also have gas-filled bladders to lift their fronds up to the surface.

SEAWEED FARMING Island communities have always harvested the bounty of their coastal waters by fishing. In some places, people now look to the sea for its farming potential. The cultivation of the seaweed eucheuma started in the Philippines in the 1970s and has spread to Indonesia. It is a source of the food additive carrageenan, added to frozen meat to aid moisture retention, and also used to improve clarity in vinegar, wine and beer. Pacific islanders, notably in Fiji and Kiribati, have recently begun growing the similar kappaphycus seaweed.

HARVEST FROM THE SEA
An Indonesian seaweed farmer gathers his crop at low tide, before the waves come pouring back in again.

BEACHCOMBERS Many crabs – including these ghost crabs on the coast of Kenya – live by scouring the strand line for dead animal matter washed up by the tides.

FILTER FEEDERS

RATHER THAN MOVING AROUND IN SEARCH OF ALGAE OR ANIMAL PREY, many creatures that live near the shore let the sea bring their food to them. They spend their adult lives fixed to one spot, sifting their meals from the water. The constant movement of water in the tidal zone ensures that they never go short, the tides bringing in fresh supplies twice a day. This means that filter feeders can live in greater concentrations in the tidal zone than elsewhere. The beds of mussels and barnacles that coat rocky shores are testament to the richness of their habitat.

Staying put has other advantages, too, when living in the tidal zone. Rough seas often batter the shores and take their toll on animals there. Filter feeders fixed to one place can weather the worst of the storms without being smashed against rocks or washed away. If necessary they can pull in their delicate feeding apparatus to prevent it getting damaged.

Legs and siphons

Coastal filter feeders have a variety of ingenious mechanisms for obtaining food. Barnacles, for instance, have modified legs covered with tiny bristles. When the tide is in, they swipe their feathery legs through the water, pulling them in periodically to remove the particles trapped by the hairs. This feeding apparatus hints at their free-swimming ancestry: barnacles are actually crustaceans, more closely related to shrimps and prawns than to most other filter-feeding shellfish.

Mussels, on the other hand, are bivalve molluscs – creatures with hinged shells made up of two separate halves. They feed by sucking water in through a tube called a siphon and driving it through their sievelike gills. As well as catching plankton and other tiny food particles, the gills extract oxygen from the water as it flows over them. The water is then squirted out through another siphon and the cycle starts all over again.

Although mussels live fixed to rocky shores, most bivalve molluscs inhabit mud or sand. A few, such as scallops, sit on the surface, but the majority, including cockles, nut shells, razor shells and tellins, bury themselves out of sight of predators. Many have a muscular foot which anchors them, but also allows limited movement. Nearly all of them live by filter feeding, pushing up their siphons, periscope-like, through the sediment to reach the water above. Although hidden, they live in huge numbers in the sediments exposed at low tide.

Filter-feeder fortresses

Being buried in mud or sand does not protect bivalve molluscs from the probing bills of waders. Nor, for that matter, does clinging to rocks. Despite its name, the oystercatcher thrives on rocky shores on a diet of mussels, prising them open with its powerful bill or hammering its way in.

There is, however, one bivalve filter feeder that has solved the problem of predation by waders. Known as the common piddock, it actually lives within the rock, sticking its siphon out to feed and pulling it back in again as soon as danger threatens. The piddock first settles on a rock as a free-swimming larva, then it tunnels into it using toothlike projections on the rear of its shell. As it grows, it enlarges the burrow around itself but the circular hole for its siphon remains the same size.

Worms and sponges

Many worms live by sifting edible particles from the water. Fan worms form tubes of calcium carbonate or cemented sand around their bodies, sticking out the feathered ends that they use to feed like tiny, colourful Christmas trees. The least shadow sends them shrinking back into their tubes for protection. Although fan worms are found throughout the world's oceans, they are most common in the waters along shores.

Perhaps the simplest filter feeders of all are the various species of sponge. Their entire bodies act as a feeding mechanism. They suck water in through the holes in their surface, sift it and then pump it back out again. Sponges are among the most primitive animals of all, with no true tissues. Their structure is so simple that even if they are broken up by being pushed through a sieve underwater, they will gradually reassemble themselves.

LITTLE STINGERS Sea anemones, such as this snakeslock, can tolerate exposure to air by pulling in their tentacles to help to conserve moisture.

STICKING POWER IN THE SURF ZONE, A STRONG GRIP CAN SAVE YOUR LIFE, AND LIMPETS HAVE ONE OF THE TIGHTEST GRIPS IN THE ANIMAL KINGDOM, CLINGING FIRMLY TO ROCKS THROUGH THE FIERCEST STORMS. When the tide is in, limpets loosen their hold and move around to graze on algae, but as the water starts to fall, each one returns to its home and hunkers down in preparation for exposure to air. They effectively glue themselves in place with an extremely sticky mucus.

Limpets are gastropod molluscs, members of the same group as slugs and snails. Like all gastropods, they move around on a single, large foot, leaving a trail of mucus as they go. This trail helps them to find their way home; as the tide falls, a limpet simply follows its trail back to its starting point. Each one has its own particular resting place on the rocks, and returns to the same spot twice a day throughout its adult life. Over time, its shell wears away a groove in the rock, making for an extremely snug fit. This helps the limpet to retain water beneath its shell, which is vital to its survival once the tide has fallen.

If a wave hits a limpet while it is moving around in the surf, it protects itself from being knocked off by pulling itself tight against the surface of the rock. The crashing water simply rushes over the low, conical shell. The speed of this reaction is incredibly fast and appears almost instantaneous to the naked eye of an observer. As soon as the wave has passed, the limpet unclamps itself and continues on its journey.

Many other gastropods live along rocky shores, but few have the sticking power of limpets. The more snail-like periwinkles stay underwater whenever possible. If caught out by the falling tide, however, they pull their shells tight against the rocks wherever they are.

LIMPET

PHYLUM Mollusca
CLASS Gastropoda
ORDER Patellogastropoda (limpets)
SPECIES *Patella vulgata*
(common limpet)
SIZE Shell up to 6 cm across
AVERAGE WEIGHT 25 g
DIET Algae
HABITAT Rocky coastlines
PULLING POWER 25 newtons

VITAL STATISTICS

NATURE'S POWERS

CRAWLING TO SAFETY Loggerhead turtles break out of their eggs unaided, then the hatchlings wriggle down the beach.

BREEDING WITH THE TIDES

SOME MARINE ANIMALS LEAVE THE SEA TO LAY THEIR EGGS ON BEACHES. Turtles do this because of their ancestral heritage. Many millions of years ago, these ocean reptiles evolved from land-living relatives, who laid eggs designed to incubate and hatch out of water.

Turtles are clumsy and slow-moving when they leave the water. For them, crawling up a beach involves a huge exertion, but they have to do it to ensure that their eggs remain dry. In order to minimise the effort and strain on their bodies, most turtles time their egg-laying to coincide with spring tides. The females gather off favourite beaches, waiting for the New or Full Moon and nightfall to make their massed landings. Laying in darkness helps to protect the eggs from the attentions of scavengers, particularly birds, which might otherwise steal them. Each female digs a pit into which she lays her eggs. Once she has finished laying, which may take hours, she covers up the eggs with sand and returns to the sea, leaving the eggs to incubate and hatch alone.

Living fossils

Horseshoe crabs also lay their eggs on beaches to give their offspring a better chance of surviving. Horseshoes are not really crabs at all, but have their own group in animal classification, intermediate between crustaceans and arachnids, such as scorpions and spiders. They have been around for so long they are sometimes called living fossils, and they have spawned in the same way for millions of years.

Every year they drag their armoured bodies in huge numbers onto favoured beaches. In most places, they concentrate their efforts at night around the spring tides, but unlike turtles, horseshoe crabs lay their eggs between the high and low tide marks. The females dig shallow pits in the sand or shingle and deposit their eggs into them. These are then fertilised by the

PRIMEVAL SCENE Horseshoe crabs emerge from the sea to spawn on a beach in the USA's Delaware Bay. They have barely changed in form and habit since before the time of the dinosaurs.

males before being covered up. The eggs lie in the sediment for around five weeks before hatching. The young stay where they are until the next spring tide, or sometimes the one after it, then they scramble up to the surface and into the water and swim vigorously out to sea.

Beaching fish

In California, fish called grunion use a similar tactic. Grunion regularly fling themselves onto beaches, and the timing of these 'runs' is linked to the lunar cycle, occurring two to six days after every spring tide from March to September. With each breaking wave, the grunions swim, wriggle and flip as far up the shore as possible. The females then dig their tails down into the sand to release their eggs, which are fertilised by attendant males. The males immediately wriggle their way back to the water, but the females have to wait until the next wave.

Grunion eggs develop in the sand and hatch during the next spring tide, allowing the young fish to swim straight into the sea. If the waves of that tide fail to reach them, the eggs can extend their incubation and delay hatching for another four weeks.

South Sea spawning

Not all creatures whose spawning coincides with the lunar cycle leave the sea to do so. In the waters off some South Pacific islands, palolo worms spawn en masse in October and November. The egg or sperm-laden rear half of each worm breaks off and wriggles to the surface, an event eagerly anticipated by the islanders, who consider the worms a delicacy. The exact link between the tides and the spawning is not firmly established. Some maintain that it happens three days after the New Moon, others that it follows the Full Moon by around seven days.

Better understood is the link between lunar cycles and the spawning of corals on Australia's Great Barrier Reef. Almost a week after the Full Moon in October or November, these tiny animals release huge quantities of eggs and sperm into the sea. This coincides with one of the smallest neap tides, when water movement is at a minimum, ensuring that the eggs and sperm are mixed but that little washes away. The corals are also stimulated to spawn by darkness. Releasing their precious cargo at night means it is less likely to be snapped up by fish.

FISH FOR THE TAKING Fishing for grunion could not be easier. Every year, these silvery fish leave the sea to spawn on Californian shores, where they are eagerly collected by local people.

CORAL REEFS

CORAL REEFS ARE THE RICHEST OF ALL OCEAN HABITATS. They provide homes for such a dazzling variety of life they have been called the rainforests of the sea, and the comparison is a good one. Like rainforests, coral reefs are found mainly in the tropics, and their bounty is generated within them, rather than drawn from their surroundings. Paradoxically, the waters in which they thrive are generally low in nutrients, the crystal clarity testifying to the lack of plankton.

Like rainforests, coral reefs grow with energy trapped from the Sun. They consist of stony structures built by countless tiny polyps – simple animals that look like miniature sea anemones (to which they are closely related) and contain algae within their tissues. Each coral polyp lives partly on the carbohydrates that the algae generate by photosynthesis, and partly on food that it catches itself from the water with its tentacles, which shoot out tiny, poison-filled barbs.

How reefs grow

Most corals in coral reefs produce calcium carbonate. They lay down this hard, chalky substance around their bodies, forming a kind of collective external skeleton. Different species produce these structures in different ways, leading to a variety of shapes. Some resemble antlers, others giant brains. Many form large platelike structures, while others grow in whorls or like clumps of cigars. Growing beside and on top of one another, they form the reef itself. Soft corals, which do not produce calcium carbonate, look more like plants and sway with the flow of the water.

Corals grow on solid surfaces. Free-swimming larvae attach themselves to hard objects, where they grow into polyps, which start to lay down cups of calcium carbonate. As the polyps get older, they lift themselves slightly out of these cups,

REEF CREATURES Moray eels hide in crevices between coral heads, only emerging during the day to frighten off intruders. Like many reef predators, they hunt at night, when their prey is less alert.

CORAL PATTERN In this typical 'spur-and-groove' reef formation off the Florida Keys, channels of sand – the grooves – separate the finger-like spurs of coral.

leaving space which they then fill with a new layer of calcium carbonate. New polyps bud off from the original settler polyp, and the chalky skeletons grow gradually into the structures we recognise as reefs.

Hard corals grow slowly, between about 3 mm and 10 cm a year, depending on the species. But they can grow for an extremely long time. While individual polyps come and go, colonies may survive for hundreds of years. The largest hard corals may be as much as 3 m across and 1000 years old. The reefs that these corals form can be truly enormous. The largest of all, the Great Barrier Reef, stretches for more than 1900 km off the north-eastern coast of Australia. It began forming 500 000 years ago.

Coral reefs need sea temperatures of at least 18°C to grow. The most northerly large reefs are around the Hawaiian islands and Honshu in Japan. In the Southern Hemisphere, they reach as far as the tropic of Capricorn, growing off Tonga and the Solomon Islands.

Fringing reefs and barrier reefs

Corals are quick to colonise suitable new sites – they soon appear on ships sunk in shallow waters, for example. As long as there is enough light, they are able to grow, and in the clearest tropical waters they may be found as far down as 70 m.

Their need for light means that they are most common near to shores, although they also grow on rocky outcrops farther out to sea. When volcanic activity creates new islands in the ocean, coral reefs soon begin to form around them. Coral reefs that cling to coastlines in this way are known as fringing reefs. Barrier reefs shadow coastlines a little farther offshore. The Belize Barrier Reef in the western Caribbean, for example, runs almost parallel to that country's beaches but is separated from them by a distance of several kilometres.

Atolls are the remains of fringing reefs that formed around volcanic islands and have survived, even though the islands themselves have long since subsided back into the sea. Most are either circular or oval, their shape giving away their past. Atolls themselves may form broken rings of new, smaller islands, built from sand or other sediment trapped by the coral. These desert islands surround shallow lagoons, containing their own rich communities of corals and other marine life.

DOUBLE VISION Pacific double-saddle butterfly fish cruise over a coral reef off Palau in Micronesia. Coral reefs are both the most productive and most colourful habitats in the ocean.

An endangered habitat

Coral reefs are dynamic but fragile structures that can die back as quickly as they grow. Violent storms and the constant motion of the sea can erode them, or bury them beneath sediment like oases lost to the shifting sands of a desert.

More immediate threats to coral reefs come from human activity – being so close to the land makes them vulnerable. Coastal development can increase freshwater runoff, driving sediments and pollutants into the sea. Increased sediment in the water cuts down light levels, which can cause 'bleaching' – a stress-related condition that causes corals to lose the algae in their tissues and die. Sudden rises in water temperature, which have been linked to El Niño events, also cause bleaching.

Other threats include cyanide and dynamite fishing. Divers use liquid cyanide when collecting reef fish for aquariums and the live seafood market. While it only stuns the fish, it kills coral. Dynamite fishing is even more destructive. Explosives are dropped into the water to kill fish, which then float to the surface. In some parts of South-east Asia, whole reefs have been destroyed by this illegal activity.

LIFE WITHIN A REEF

THERE ARE WELL OVER 2000 DIFFERENT SPECIES OF CORAL, BUT THEIR DIVERSITY IS AS NOTHING COMPARED WITH THE VARIETY OF LIFE THAT THEY SUPPORT. Coral reefs are home to a vast number of animals: according to some estimates, a quarter of all the species that live in the sea – an incredible statistic considering the relatively small area of ocean that coral reefs cover.

Anyone diving or snorkelling on coral reefs is struck by the sheer teeming abundance of animals there, and bold colours and patterns are a distinctive feature of many coral reef animals. While in most habitats creatures use camouflage to avoid being noticed, here they seem to glow like beacons. The evolutionary advantages of this are hard to pin down. The best explanation scientists can offer has to do with identification. With so many species in the same place, a distinctive outfit helps creatures to find others of their own kind.

Of course, not all coral reef animals are bold and garish. Some go to extraordinary lengths not to be seen. Many frogfish, for example, look almost exactly like pieces of coral or sponges, their camouflage so complete that they are invisible until they move. Frogfish are predators that hunt by ambush, staying motionless until prey wanders or swims within reach. When it does, they react with lightning speed, opening their mouths

suddenly to suck their victims in. The talent that frogfish have for staying hidden is enhanced in some species by an amazing ability to change colour and pattern. As they move through the reef and find different sites for ambush, their bodies slowly alter until they perfectly match their new background.

While frogfish use camouflage to hunt, other creatures hide to avoid being eaten. Many shrimps and crabs blend in with the corals they live on, growing spines and other protuberances to match not just their host's colour but also its shape.

Reef food web

The food web of a reef is incredibly complex but centres largely around the corals themselves. Just like plants on land, these animals are the primary producers, harnessing energy from the Sun through the microscopic algae in their bodies.

For other creatures, they are an abundant food source, never hard to find. Getting hold of coral, however, can be a challenge, since individual polyps are small and quick to shrink back into their stony casing. Some fish defeat them with precision and speed. The coral butterfly fish, for example, darts in with its pointed snout to nip off polyps faster than they can retreat. Other species use brute force. Named for their tough, horny beaks, parrotfish bite off chunks of coral, crunching it up with powerful teeth. They swallow both the polyps and their ground-up homes, ejecting the latter as fine coral sand.

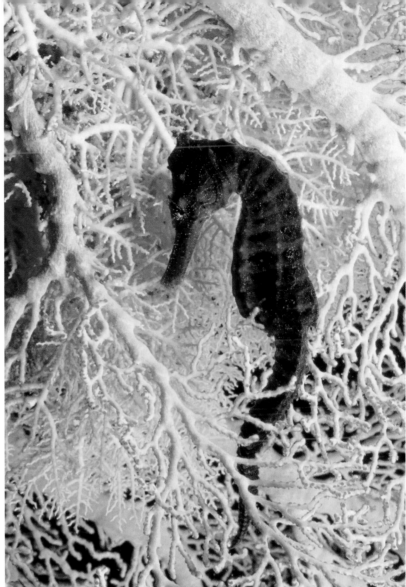

BRIGHT AND BEAUTIFUL Diagonal-banded sweetlips on Australia's Great Barrier Reef (opposite). These fish are most active at night, when they scour the reef for invertebrates.

GRIPPING TAIL Uniquely among fish, seahorses (right) have a prehensile tail, which they use to hold on to coral branches to stop themselves being washed away.

Some fish feed on the films of algae which grow on the surface of corals. Tang fish and surgeonfish scour the reefs in colourful, coordinated schools, stopping en masse to graze wherever they find algae patches growing. Many other small fish feed on the reef's invertebrate inhabitants, poking into nooks and crannies to find their food.

By day, a coral reef seems a place of great tranquillity. Night-time is when most of the big predators come out, including moray eels which emerge from their lairs as darkness falls. These huge fish, some up to 2.5 m long and as thick as a man's leg, have large, backward-curving teeth to hold on to struggling prey. Most octopuses also hunt at night. Like moray eels, they spend the daylight hours hidden in crevices or under rocks. Octopuses have soft, muscular bodies, allowing them to squeeze through surprisingly small gaps. They capture prey with their powerful tentacles, drawing it in to the mouth for a killing bite from a venomous 'beak'.

Perhaps the most fearsome nocturnal predators are the sharks. By day, black-tipped and white-tipped reef sharks swim lazily off the edge of the reef, only occasionally making forays into it, scattering fish as they go. At night, however, their attacks become more concentrated, as large numbers roam over the reef, using their electrical senses to locate hidden prey. The fish they hunt use sight to find their food and so are active by day. At dusk, most find somewhere to hide and go into a sleeplike torpor. The sharks either pull them physically from their hiding places or drive them out into open water, where they are quickly snapped up.

Feeding on plankton

Not all reef dwellers are hunters or eat coral or algae. Despite the low levels of plankton in the water, some filter feeders manage to live in coral reefs, including many species of fan worms and sponges. Although corals themselves are not, technically, filter feeders because they do not sift their food from the water, they do capture planktonic animals to supplement the nutrients provided by their internal algae. Anything that touches the frilly tentacles of the coral is shot by nematocysts, specialised stinging cells very like those of their free-living cousins, the jellyfish.

One group of animals takes advantage of these stinging cells. Nudibranchs, or sea slugs, eat a variety of foods but many reef species feed on coral polyps. Rather than digesting the stinging cells, they embed them in the surface of their own bodies for their own defence. With this battery of poisonous barbs in place, sea slugs are left alone by most predators and move boldly over the reef in the broad light of day.

OUT FOR LUNCH Coral polyps feed on tiny organisms and other edible particles in the water, which they catch with long, extended tentacles.

GIA

NTS 5

THE WORLD'S BIGGEST ANIMALS ALL LIVE IN THE OCEANS. Seawater produces vast quantities of food that can sustain real-life leviathans such as this bowhead whale. The bowhead has the largest mouth of any creature on Earth. Wide open, it is as big as a garage – a minibus could park in it with room to spare. Like many of the biggest whales, the bowhead eats tiny prey, sifting it from the water with plates of hornlike material called baleen. Other ocean giants are more ferocious predators. Sperm whales, orcas and great white sharks hunt large animals, killing their prey with terrifying power. Some soft-bodied invertebrate sea creatures have evolved to monster size, too, including the giant squid with eyes the size of dinner plates and jellyfish with trailing tentacles that are longer than most trees are tall.

THE BIG CATCH

MARINE ANIMALS CAN GROW TO SUCH INCREDIBLE SIZES BECAUSE THE WATER SUPPORTS THEIR HUGE BULK AND WEIGHT. Buoyed up by water, they feel the effects of gravity much less than animals on land.

Being large has definite advantages in the open ocean, where there are no obstacles to movement. The sheer size of the biggest animals makes them almost immune to predation, while their huge muscle mass enables them to travel long distances between often scattered concentrations of food.

Air-breathing divers

It may seem strange, but the biggest of all ocean creatures cannot live continuously underwater. Whales breathe air and so they have to return regularly to the surface. To minimise the inconvenience, they fill their enormous lungs to capacity, taking several breaths before diving. Their bodies have also evolved to operate on lower levels of oxygen than those of most land-living animals.

Some whale species can stay underwater for more than an hour at a time, only exhaling through their blowholes when they return to the surface. Water vapour and tiny droplets of mucous in their breath make these exhalations, or 'blows', visible from a distance. The height, direction and shape of the blow depend on the position and shape of the blowhole, which may have one or two nostrils. This means that different species can be identified by their blows.

Streamlined hunters

Like us, whales are mammals – warm-blooded animals that feed their young on milk. They evolved from an ancestor of the hoofed mammals around 50 million years ago, eventually becoming completely adapted for life in the sea. Sharks, in contrast, have always been sea-dwellers. These ancient fish – the largest in the sea – have been cruising the oceans for at least 400 million years. Today, sharks include some massive predators, but they were once even bigger. Before its extinction over a million years ago, Megalodon ('great tooth') grew to 15 m long and had triangular teeth measuring 17 cm from base to tip.

Almost all sharks are active predators, hunting a wide range of prey. Many of the larger species are highly streamlined, cutting through the water like living torpedoes and powering into their victims at speed. Pectoral fins at their sides act like wings, giving them lift in the water, while the triangular dorsal fin on the back works like a keel to provide stability.

Sharks locate their prey using a combination of senses: sensitive hearing, smell and the ability to detect electrical currents and pressure changes in the water. Most species also have excellent vision, which they use during the attack. Once they home in on a victim, there is little chance of escape. Their size, speed and power make sharks hard to outrun and even harder to resist physically. Even other large ocean creatures, such as manta rays and small whales, can fall prey to them.

BIG FISH, LITTLE FISH
A bronze whaler shark charges into a bait ball of sardines off South Africa. Sharks are among the most primitive fish in the sea, having changed little in body form in 400 million years.

SCOOPING UP FOOD The southern right whale feeds on small fish and krill. Like most of the largest whales, it has plates of baleen hanging from its upper jaw, which it uses to filter its prey from the seawater.

SHARKS

THE LARGEST AND MOST POWERFUL FISH IN THE SEA, sharks have a fearsome reputation as man-eaters. In reality, only the larger species, those over 3 m long, pose any potential threat to humans. The vast majority of sharks are as wary of people as we are of them. Of the 368 species of shark in the ocean, 42 have been known to attack humans and just 11 of those are known to have killed humans. Even then, people are not their preferred food. The common view of sharks as monsters says more about our own species than it does about theirs. The dangerous few get all the publicity – but there is no denying that these few exist.

The great white shark

The most dangerous of all sharks to humans is the great white, the largest predatory shark. Its tendency to hunt for seals and sea lions along coastlines often brings it into contact with people, particularly surfers. It used to be thought that great whites

> **'Great whites are curious and investigative animals ... when [they] bite something unfamiliar to them ... they are looking for tactile evidence about what it is.'**
>
> **Aidan Martin**
> **ReefQuest Centre for Shark Research, Vancouver**

SHARK SURVIVOR *Bethany Hamilton was attacked by a great white in Hawaii. Attacks on humans are rare; surfers are probably targeted out of curiosity.*

JAWS OF DEATH The great white shark attacks its prey with mouth wide open and eyes rolled back in its head for protection. Its huge teeth have serrated edges like carving knives.

mistook surfers on their boards for seals, which also play in the waves. But the methods the sharks use to attack seals and people are very different. When hunting seals or sea lions, great whites tend to power up into their prey from below, breaking flesh and crushing bone with a single, massive bite. Studies of attacks on surfers – some of which have been captured on video – show a less aggressive behaviour pattern. The sharks approach surfers in an almost leisurely manner, biting once and then usually swimming away. Aidan Martin, director of Vancouver's ReefQuest Centre for Shark Research, explains: 'Great whites are curious and investigative animals ... when [they] bite something unfamiliar to them ... they are looking for tactile evidence about what it is.'

So it seems that although great whites have killed more people than any other shark species, these deaths are not the result of feeding behaviour. Backing this up is the fact that many surfers attacked by these massive animals have escaped with only minor puncture wounds.

Bull and tiger sharks

The two other large species most often implicated in attacks on humans are less choosy about their food. Bull sharks grow to more than 3 m long and are found the world over around tropical and subtropical coastlines. Unlike most sharks, they enter estuaries and rivers – they have been reported in the Amazon and Mississippi hundreds of kilometres from the sea – and have been known to kill people in shallow water. Their usual diet includes fish, turtles, birds, crustaceans and dolphins.

Tiger sharks are second only to the great white in terms of numbers of attacks on people. They are common in tropical and subtropical coastal waters worldwide, and have been recorded farther afield as well – even as far north as Iceland. Tiger sharks regularly grow in excess of 5m and have earned themselves a reputation as 'dustbins of the sea' because they will eat almost anything. The stomach contents of landed individuals have included bottles of wine, car tyres and even unexploded munitions.

Tools of predation

Most sharks are predators that feed by slicing chunks off their prey or swallowing it whole. As they do not chew they need a powerful digestive system, and most species have extremely acidic digestive juices which can even dissolve bone. The tools sharks use to kill and eat are, of course, their formidable teeth. These have serrated edges and are incredibly sharp, designed for cutting through prey rather than holding onto it.

Unlike most vertebrates, which have just one or two sets of teeth in a lifetime, sharks continually grow and replace their teeth. As the teeth age, they gradually move towards the front of the jaws, eventually falling out or becoming lodged in prey, to be replaced by newer ones directly behind them. This continuous regeneration means that a shark may have more than 100 teeth in its mouth at one time, in several uneven rows. Long-lived species may get through as many as 20 000 teeth.

The classic image of the shark is of the streamlined hunter, restlessly roaming open waters in search of its next meal. Most sharks fit this description quite well – in fact, many species are forced to roam as they must keep moving in order to breathe. Unlike most other fish, which can pump water over their gills when they are not moving, many shark species need to swim through water with their gill slits open in order to change the water around their gills. The great white shark is one such species. Constant swimming is also vital if a shark is not to sink. Unlike other fish, sharks do not have a swimbladder, so they have no way of adjusting their buoyancy in water. Instead, they use their pectoral fins like the wings of an aeroplane to give them lift, but this only works with continuous propulsion from the tail.

SHARP SENSES

SHARKS' EYES ARE TEN TIMES MORE SENSITIVE THAN OUR OWN IN DIM LIGHT, enabling them to see prey clearly even in relatively deep water. At the moment of impact many species, including the great white, roll their eyes back in their heads for protection. Some have a third eyelid, called a nictitating membrane, which they close to protect their eyes.

Although vision is important to most sharks, it is just one of several senses at their disposal. Perhaps the most unusual is their ability to pick up electrical pulses. This enables some sharks to pinpoint prey even when they cannot see it. The slightest muscular movement generates tiny electrical currents, so a shark at close range can even detect a fish lying still in complete darkness, the fish betraying its presence by the tiny current produced by its beating heart.

The ampullae of Lorenzini

A shark detects electrical currents through small, jelly-filled pits in its snout, called ampullae of Lorenzini. In the hammerhead shark, these are distributed across the entire underside of its 'hammer', leading some scientists to suggest that the head's unusual shape is itself an adaptation for hunting. Great hammerheads are major predators of stingrays, which often lie partially buried under sand for protection. These sharks have been observed cruising slowly over the sea bottom, swinging their heads in broad arcs like metal detectors. When they locate a hidden stingray, they turn back suddenly and dive into the sediment to scoop out their meal.

Sharks also have a very keen sense of smell that enables them to home in on potential meals from some distance. They are famous for their ability to detect blood in water, picking it up from as far as 500 m away, then following its increasing concentration to the source. A shark's sense of smell is so acute it can detect one part of blood in 100 million parts of water. Even more sensitive is the shark's hearing, which can pick up the low-frequency vibrations made by injured fish more than 2 km distant. Closer in, the shark uses receptor cells along its lateral line to add yet more detail to the picture. These can detect pressure changes in water made by a struggling animal from over 200 m away.

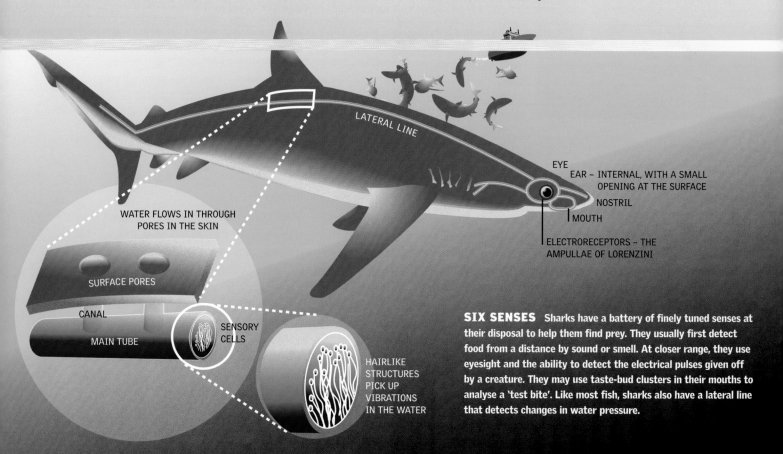

WATER FLOWS IN THROUGH PORES IN THE SKIN

SURFACE PORES

CANAL

MAIN TUBE

SENSORY CELLS

HAIRLIKE STRUCTURES PICK UP VIBRATIONS IN THE WATER

LATERAL LINE

EYE

EAR – INTERNAL, WITH A SMALL OPENING AT THE SURFACE

NOSTRIL

MOUTH

ELECTRORECEPTORS – THE AMPULLAE OF LORENZINI

SIX SENSES Sharks have a battery of finely tuned senses at their disposal to help them find prey. They usually first detect food from a distance by sound or smell. At closer range, they use eyesight and the ability to detect the electrical pulses given off by a creature. They may use taste-bud clusters in their mouths to analyse a 'test bite'. Like most fish, sharks also have a lateral line that detects changes in water pressure.

WITH A VAST, SLEEK BODY AND TEETH LIKE STEAK KNIVES, THE GREAT WHITE SHARK IS AN AWESOME PREDATOR.

This monster fish cruises the coastal waters of most of the world's oceans, occasionally travelling as far north as the British Isles. Its main prey are marine mammals, particularly seals and sea lions, which it kills with its devastatingly powerful bite. Victims are picked out from below as silhouettes near the surface, then hit with incredible force. Not all feeding attempts are successful, and prey is not always killed instantly. Struggling victims are often left to bleed in order to weaken them before the shark swims back in to feed. Although fearsome, even a great white can be injured by a sea lion's teeth or the flailing claws of its flippers.

Great white sharks are the biggest predatory fish in the sea. They can reach at least 6 m in length, and there are reports of 9 m individuals. Females grow larger than the males, and a fully grown adult female can weigh more than 3 tonnes. Despite their size and notoriety, great white sharks are little studied. What is known is that some individuals return to the same sections of coast year after year, although they rarely stay in one area for more than a few months at a time. Their breeding behaviour has never been observed, but in late spring to early summer females give birth to an average of eight or nine fully formed young, each measuring about 1.5 m in length. They leave the mother immediately after birth.

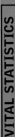

VITAL STATISTICS

LATIN NAME: *Carcharodon carcharias*
COMMON NAMES: Great white shark, white pointer
LENGTH: Up to 7 m, possibly longer
MAXIMUM WEIGHT: About 3 tonnes
LIFESPAN: Unknown – estimates vary from 20 to 50 years
PREY: Mainly seals and sea lions, although fish, squid and occasionally humans are also taken
PREDATORS: Human beings, sperm whales, orcas and other great white sharks
CLOSEST RELATIVES: Mako sharks and porbeagles (salmon sharks)

NATURE'S POWERS

DOCILE TITANS & SWIFT KILLERS

THE WORLD'S OCEANS ARE HOME TO 368 SPECIES OF SHARK. They range from 18 m giants to creatures smaller than trout. Most are predators, hunting fish and other sea life to survive, but the two largest species are filter feeders. The whale shark and basking shark live on plankton, scooping it up in their gaping mouths and filtering it from the water with their gills.

The whale shark is found mainly in tropical and subtropical waters, while the basking shark inhabits more temperate seas. Basking sharks are regularly seen off Britain and North America, north of Cape Cod. They also inhabit the northern Pacific and similar latitudes south of the Equator. Although not as big as the whale shark, basking sharks are still massive creatures. The largest measured was 11 m long and weighed almost 4 tonnes. Observations made in the field suggest that they can grow even bigger, reaching lengths of more than 13 m – longer than a double-decker bus. Whale sharks and basking sharks are slow-moving, even docile fish with tiny teeth just a few millimetres long, which makes them very much exceptions to the rule among sharks. Most other sharks are formidable predators built for speed.

Large predators

Several predatory species grow to lengths of more than 4 m. After the great white, the largest is the Greenland or sleeper shark, which reaches 6.5 m long (see page 154). Another giant is the great hammerhead shark. It can grow up to 6 m long. Unlike most hammerhead species, the great hammerhead spends much of its time alone, scouring the tropical and temperate coastal waters it inhabits for prey. Its 'hammer' may help it to detect hidden fish, but some scientists argue that it acts as a hydrofoil or, by separating the nostrils, improves the shark's ability to pinpoint prey by smell. It probably serves all of these functions. Which one originally spurred the evolution of the curiously shaped head will probably remain a mystery.

Smaller killers

Of course, not all sharks are giants. In fact, the vast majority are simply large fish, ranging from 1 m to 3 m long. They are only as big as they need to be to tackle the creatures they feed on. However, even a 1 m shark can look fearsome underwater, and its relatively small size is no guarantee it will not attack. Some divers have been attacked and injured by 1 m long nurse sharks and dogfish, although such incidents are rare.

One small shark survives by attacking creatures much larger than itself. Known as the cookie-cutter shark, it bites circular chunks from the skin of whales and other unsuspecting prey. Cookie-cutters, like most sharks, pick up small electrical

currents, and this has led them to attack and disable telephone cables on the seabed. They also attack submarines – whether they are drawn to them by the currents given off by the metal hulls or whether they mistake them for whales is not known.

Lantern sharks also have unusual feeding habits. They grow to just 25 cm long, and are believed to hunt in packs. They feed on animals much bigger than themselves, but kill and dismember prey rather than merely biting off chunks. A deep-water species, they hunt squid in darkness, locating prey with a highly developed sense of smell and sensitivity to the electrical pulses generated by muscle activity. A squid may be hounded by several lantern sharks; once one has attacked, the rest charge in.

DIFFERENT DIETS Most sharks, such as the scalloped hammerhead (above), are active predators that hunt large prey. A few, however, are filter feeders. The whale shark (below) is the world's largest fish, weighing up to 15 tonnes. It lives mainly on a diet of plankton, with krill and other small sea creatures, which it sifts from the water using rakers in its gill slits.

TOP PREDATOR The tiger shark is one of the largest active predators in the oceans and second only to the great white shark in terms of danger to humans. Like the great white, it often hunts large prey near the shore, which brings it into contact with people. Adult tiger sharks average 3-4 m long, but some very large individuals exceed 5.5 m.

WHALES

ONE OF THE BIGGEST CREATURES THAT HAS EVER EXISTED ON EARTH STILL LIVES IN THE OCEANS TODAY. The blue whale outweighs any dinosaur ever discovered and is several times heavier than the whale shark, the world's biggest fish. Even the second-largest whale, the fin whale, can grow to more than 26 m long and weigh over 95 tonnes – an animal the length of a basketball court and 2 m longer than a tennis court – with a mass equivalent to 1300 people. Like the whale shark, these two giant creatures are filter feeders, consuming vast quantities of relatively tiny prey.

Whales belong to the order of marine mammals called cetaceans. They are generally divided into two groups: toothed whales, which include sperm whales, killer whales (or orcas), dolphins and porpoises; and baleen whales. Instead of teeth, baleen whales have plates of a hornlike substance, called baleen, which they use like a sieve to separate their food from the water. Most of the largest whales, including blue and fin whales, are baleen whales. They once cruised the oceans in enormous numbers, but now are comparatively few due to the effects of commercial whaling. Baleen, also known as whalebone (although it is not, in fact, bone), was once used to strengthen corsets and as umbrella ribs, while whale oil was used in the manufacture of products ranging from soap and cosmetics to glycerin and linoleum. Today, whales are protected but even so their numbers are recovering only slowly.

THERE SHE BLOWS The blue whale (opposite), like all whales, is a mammal and must breathe air to survive. It inhales and exhales through a blowhole on the top of the head with nostrils that are opened and pulled shut by powerful muscles.

SOCIABLE HUNTERS Sperm whales travel the ocean in groups. Females form harems led by a dominant male and travel with their young. Adult males without harems live in bachelor groups and challenge dominant males in spring and summer for the right to mate.

SPERM WHALES

Another giant that has suffered greatly at the hands of whalers is the sperm whale, the fifth-largest whale, whose head contains a wax called spermaceti, once in great demand for making candles. It was this species that inspired Herman Melville's classic novel *Moby Dick*. The sperm whale – a toothed rather than a baleen whale – is the largest predatory animal on Earth. Adult bull sperm whales can measure 18 m long and weigh up to 50 tonnes.

As well as being the world's largest predator, the sperm whale holds several other records. It has the biggest brain of any animal, weighing 8 kg. Despite being only the fifth-largest whale, this is not surprising as predators generally have larger brains than herbivores or filter feeders, probably reflecting their more complex behaviour patterns. Sperm whales also dive deeper than any other air-breathing animal. Tagged individuals have been recorded at depths of 2 km and indirect evidence suggests that they can go even deeper, perhaps as far as 3 km below the surface. They can hold their breath for over an hour.

Diving deep for prey

Sperm whales dive to such great depths to find their prey. Their main diet is squid, many species of which, notably the giant squid, live in the ocean's deeper waters. The giant squid is the world's largest invertebrate – it can grow to a weight of just over 2 tonnes and can be as long as the sperm whale itself. Giant squid are armed with disc-shaped suckers, each ringed with vicious, sharp-edged 'teeth'. Many sperm whales bear the scars of battle with these creatures, although the whales' thick skin and blubber means the wounds are only ever superficial.

Sperm whales are thought to find their prey in the darkness using echolocation, a technique known to be used by smaller toothed whales, such as dolphins and orcas. Sperm

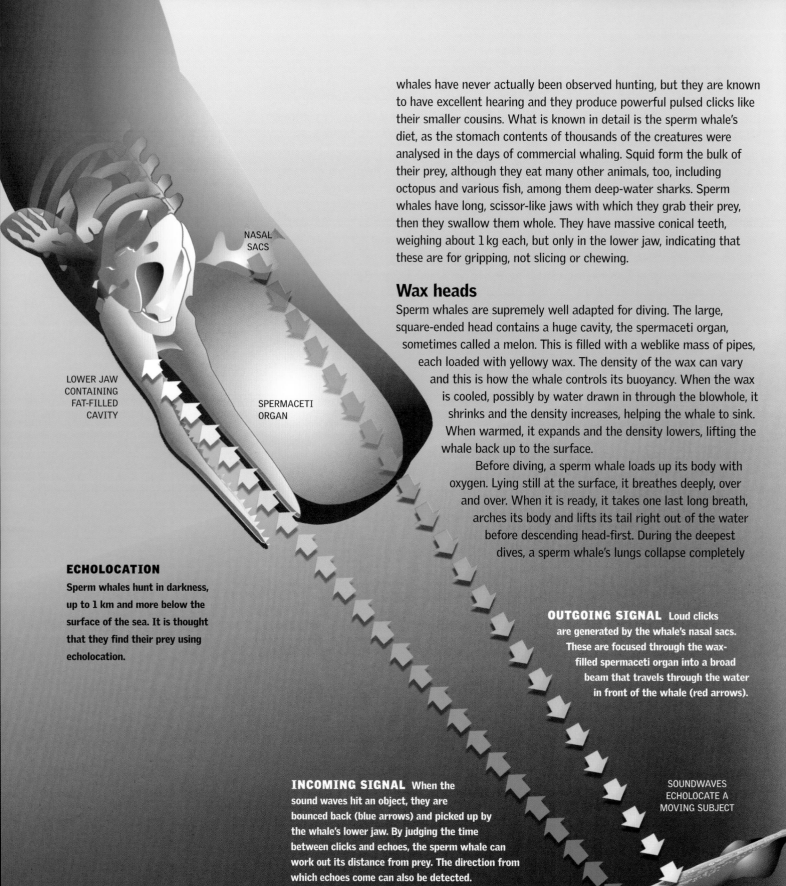

whales have never actually been observed hunting, but they are known to have excellent hearing and they produce powerful pulsed clicks like their smaller cousins. What is known in detail is the sperm whale's diet, as the stomach contents of thousands of the creatures were analysed in the days of commercial whaling. Squid form the bulk of their prey, although they eat many other animals, too, including octopus and various fish, among them deep-water sharks. Sperm whales have long, scissor-like jaws with which they grab their prey, then they swallow them whole. They have massive conical teeth, weighing about 1 kg each, but only in the lower jaw, indicating that these are for gripping, not slicing or chewing.

Wax heads

Sperm whales are supremely well adapted for diving. The large, square-ended head contains a huge cavity, the spermaceti organ, sometimes called a melon. This is filled with a weblike mass of pipes, each loaded with yellowy wax. The density of the wax can vary and this is how the whale controls its buoyancy. When the wax is cooled, possibly by water drawn in through the blowhole, it shrinks and the density increases, helping the whale to sink. When warmed, it expands and the density lowers, lifting the whale back up to the surface.

Before diving, a sperm whale loads up its body with oxygen. Lying still at the surface, it breathes deeply, over and over. When it is ready, it takes one last long breath, arches its body and lifts its tail right out of the water before descending head-first. During the deepest dives, a sperm whale's lungs collapse completely

NASAL
SACS

LOWER JAW
CONTAINING
FAT-FILLED
CAVITY

SPERMACETI
ORGAN

ECHOLOCATION
Sperm whales hunt in darkness, up to 1 km and more below the surface of the sea. It is thought that they find their prey using echolocation.

OUTGOING SIGNAL Loud clicks are generated by the whale's nasal sacs. These are focused through the wax-filled spermaceti organ into a broad beam that travels through the water in front of the whale (red arrows).

INCOMING SIGNAL When the sound waves hit an object, they are bounced back (blue arrows) and picked up by the whale's lower jaw. By judging the time between clicks and echoes, the sperm whale can work out its distance from prey. The direction from which echoes come can also be detected.

SOUNDWAVES
ECHOLOCATE A
MOVING SUBJECT

and it relies on the oxygen stored in its muscles and blood. The heartbeat slows and most body processes almost shut down as the oxygen is directed to where it is most needed, principally the brain and heart.

Family life

Unlike most large whales, sperm whales are highly social animals. Females and their calves live in close-knit family units of around 20 individuals, known as 'breeding schools', which travel and hunt together. When they reach adulthood, males leave the females and join 'bachelor schools', which generally also contain around 20 whales. Here they remain until they are large enough to challenge dominant bulls for the right to mate and lead a harem. Large sperm whale bulls without harems live solitary lives or form small groups of up to six individuals. Although sperm whales spend most of their lives in these units, they sometimes gather in much larger numbers. 'Superherds' of hundreds and even thousands of whales have been reported. The reason for these large gatherings is not known, although they may be linked to temporary concentrations of food – possibly breeding swarms of giant squid.

Sperm whales are found throughout most of the world's oceans. They are most common around submarine canyons on the edge of the continental shelf, but also occur farther out to sea, wherever food is plentiful. Because they tend to hunt large prey in deep water they are rarely seen along coasts, and when they are it is usually near steep drop-offs, where the seabed is 200 m or more beneath the surface.

Some sperm whales are residents, staying in the same relatively small area of sea for the whole of their lives. Others travel widely, generally moving towards the poles in summer and back into temperate or tropical waters as winter sets in. Large bull sperm whales may migrate to the edge of the polar ice, but females and young rarely venture so far. Adult females are significantly smaller than males, generally reaching lengths of just 11-12 m and weighing closer to 20 tonnes than 50.

Breaching whales

Despite being such large animals, sperm whales can be surprisingly agile. They often leap from the sea – a behaviour called breaching – sometimes lifting their entire bodies out of the water. More often, just a portion of the body emerges. Most breaching is performed by juveniles, particularly in rough seas, although females have been seen to breach repeatedly around large males during the breeding season, suggesting it may play a role in courtship.

Sperm whales were targeted by whalers for their spermaceti oil, but compared with most large whale species, their numbers remain relatively healthy. Estimates put the global population at over a million – a fraction of what it once was but still far from endangered.

GIANT SQUID It takes a big meal to fill up the world's largest predator, the sperm whale, but giant squid go some way towards it. Formidable hunters themselves, these huge molluscs cruise the ocean depths in search of prey, which they find with the help of the largest eyes in the animal kingdom. Very little is known about how these creatures live – most of our information comes from remains found in the stomachs of sperm whales – but occasionally one comes to the surface. The specimen below washed up on a beach in Tasmania in 2002. In 2003 one clamped itself to the hull of a yacht taking part in the round-the-world Jules Verne Trophy race. 'I saw a tentacle through a porthole,' said the skipper Olivier de Kersauson. 'It was thicker than my leg and it was really pulling the boat hard.' The squid released its grip when de Kersauson stopped the boat. The first photo of a live giant squid was taken in 2004 (see page 128).

EVERY SO OFTEN WHALES ARE WASHED UP ON BEACHES. Strandings of dead whales are easily explained: the animals die at sea and are washed onto shores by prevailing currents and tides. Much of what we know about some species has come from such beached carcasses. One species, the Longman's beaked whale, has never been seen alive and is known only from its washed-up remains. Sometimes, however, live whales appear on beaches and occasionally whole groups are stranded together.

The phenomenon of live strandings is one of the enduring mysteries of nature, though several theories have been put forward to explain it. Some scientists believe that whales use patterns in the Earth's magnetic field to help them navigate underwater. When these patterns change, as they occasionally do, the whales become disoriented and swim onto beaches by accident. Another theory is that a brain infection or other illness could confuse a whale's sense of direction. Such an illness in just one animal could cause mass

If discovered in time, stranded whales can be rescued and returned to the sea. In June 2005, more than 60 false killer whales were saved after a mass stranding in Western Australia.

STRANDED

strandings in social species, where a group is thought to follow a dominant individual. A third possible explanation is that whales simply swim by accident into water that is too shallow, perhaps panicked by earthquakes or submarine landslides.

Man-induced strandings

Live strandings probably occur for many different reasons, which may vary from species to species. There is one cause, however, that is universal – and man-made. In 1985, the US Navy introduced a powerful new sonar system called SURTASS/LFA (SURveillance Towed Array Sensor System/Low Frequency Active), designed to detect 'silent' submarines from the surface. The system works using massive amplifiers to create incredibly loud sound pulses, which are fired out through a wide array of speakers. Each pulse may be 215 decibels or more – louder than a twin-engined fighter jet at takeoff. These effectively 'floodlight' the sea, showing objects other sonar systems cannot detect.

While SURTASS/LFA is effective at detecting submarines, it has been shown to have a devastating effect on whales. Mass strandings have occurred in several places where the system has been tested or used. Post-mortem examinations revealed internal bleeding around the whales' brains and ears. In some cases, entire populations of whales have disappeared from an area after testing. Whether they were all killed or just left has not been established.

The widespread deployment of SURTASS/LFA by the US Navy has recently been reined in by new legislation, although the US government added provisos aimed at bypassing this. Elsewhere in the world, other navies have developed their own LFA sonar systems. In 2004, the European Parliament called on its 25 member states to halt their deployment and use.

Rescued from the beaches

If discovered in time, stranded whales can be rescued and returned to the sea. In June 2005, more than 60 false killer whales were saved after a mass stranding in Western Australia. Hundreds of local volunteers turned out to help the 5 m long animals, which had beached themselves near the coastal town of Brusselton. They kept the whales wet with buckets of seawater until they could be pushed back into the ocean as the tide came in. Small boats were then used to guide the whales back into open water. The false killer whale is one of several toothed species that often becomes stranded.

HELPING HANDS Most types of whale have been washed up on beaches. In fact, most of what is known about some of the rarer species comes from strandings. Small coastal species make up the majority of strandings, but occasionally larger, oceanic whales become trapped. This humpback was stranded on a Brazilian beach in 2004. Despite the valiant efforts of local people to return it to the sea, it eventually died. Deprived of the buoyancy provided by deep water, a stranded whale's internal organs can be crushed by its own weight. Other threats to the creature's survival include overheating, and water or sand getting into the blowhole.

Varied hunting tactics

Killer whales feed on a wide variety of animals, though different pods tend to concentrate on different prey. Those pods that feed on fish in coastal waters are usually the largest. They work as a unit to herd shoals of fish tightly together before charging through them to feed. Some fish-eating killer whales drive their herded shoals up to the surface where they stun them by slapping the water with their tails, a behaviour known as tail-lobbing. Wherever they live, fish-eating pods are usually highly vocal, making a wide variety of whistles and clicks to keep in touch and communicate information on prey.

Pods that feed on marine mammals make far less noise. For them, stealth and surprise are important elements of a successful hunt. Mammal-eating pods are usually small, as their prey is often scattered and tends to be caught individually. Some marine mammals, such as elephant seals, provide a lot of meat for relatively little effort, but others, such as porpoises, are hard to catch and have far less flesh to be shared out.

At home the world over

After humans, killer whales are the most widely distributed mammals on Earth. They live in all of the world's oceans and range from the Arctic and Antarctic pack ice to the Equator. Most killer whale pods are concentrated in coastal waters, but they may also be seen far out to sea.

Although they are called whales, killer whales actually belong to the dolphin family, Delphinidae, which also includes melon-headed and pilot whale species. Adult male killer whales can reach over 9 m long and weigh up to 10 tonnes. Females are smaller, averaging about 6 m long. The main difference between the sexes, apart from size, is the shape of the dorsal fin. In males, it is tall and straight, measuring up to 1.8 m long; in females, it is much shorter and curved.

Like all dolphins, killer whales have conical, pointed teeth that curve slightly backwards towards the throat to help them grip prey. Killer whale teeth are much larger than those of other members of the Delphinidae family, sometimes sticking out 12 cm from the gums. Unlike sharks, which slice chunks of flesh from large prey, killer whales rip it off by gripping it between their teeth and pulling violently.

Pack hunters

Because of their coordinated group hunting behaviour, killer whales are sometimes called the wolves of the sea. They are intelligent, adaptable predators, like wolves, but they show an even greater capacity to solve problems and learn. Some pods have hunting behaviours that are unique to them or to killer whales in their particular area. For example, killer whales have been seen tipping ice floes with their heads to force seals or penguins resting on them into the water. They have also been observed playing with their prey long after it is dead, flinging it across the surface of the water with a flick of the tail.

KILLER WHALES

THE GREAT WHITE SHARK MAY BE FEARSOME BUT IT IS NOT THE TOP PREDATOR IN THE OCEANS. If any animal deserves that title, it is the killer whale, or orca. Killer whales have been filmed hunting and eating great whites. They have even been known to kill and feed on blue whales.

Killer whales are cooperative predators. They live in close-knit family groups called pods, which might contain as few as 3 or as many as 50 animals. Occasionally, these pods join with others in their area to form larger groups called herds. Killer whale pods are led by the older females, although they also contain grown-up sons. Breeding behaviour has been little studied but it is thought that mating occurs between pods rather than within them.

In some areas, individuals leave the pods they were born into when those pods reach a certain size. In others, they stay with the same pod all their lives, regardless of its size. The difference is thought to be driven by the abundance and type of food available. Some prey is too small or scattered to be shared effectively among a large pod.

DIVIDE AND CONQUER
A small pod of killer whales attack a grey whale and her calf migrating up the west coast of North America. The killer whales are undeterred by the mother's great size, and start by working to separate the two animals.

MATERNAL DEFENCE
The killer whales' intended victim is the grey whale calf. Desperate to save her offspring, the mother helps it to the surface to breathe. One swipe of her tail could seriously injure a killer whale, but the attackers are persistent and continue to harry mother and calf.

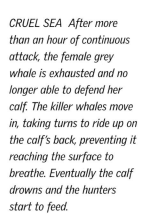

CRUEL SEA After more than an hour of continuous attack, the female grey whale is exhausted and no longer able to defend her calf. The killer whales move in, taking turns to ride up on the calf's back, preventing it reaching the surface to breathe. Eventually the calf drowns and the hunters start to feed.

BALEEN WHALES

THE WORLD'S BIGGEST ANIMALS FEED ON TINY CREATURES THOUSANDS OF TIMES SMALLER THAN THEY ARE. Baleen whales eat krill and shoaling fish, scooping huge quantities of prey from the water and trapping it in their mouths. They then use their tongues to push the water through the sievelike plates of baleen, or whalebone, that hang from their upper jaws, catching the animals in the 'mesh' of the baleen. In addition, the baleen whale species called rorquals (from the Norwegian 'rorhval', meaning groove or furrow) have great folds in the skin below their lower jaws. When they feed, the skin expands like the scooping beak of a gigantic pelican, enabling them to take in huge mouthfuls of water and food.

Baleen whales can be found throughout the world's oceans, but they are most common where prey is most heavily concentrated. In summer, they gather in large numbers around Antarctica to feed on krill. As the days lengthen, these shrimplike crustaceans form vast breeding swarms containing billions of creatures, all in their turn feeding on the phytoplankton (drifting microscopic algae) that multiplies under the summer sun. Migrating fish also attract baleen whales. In late autumn and winter off South Africa, for example, huge shoals of pilchards attract whales across large distances from the surrounding sea.

Earth's largest animals

Altogether, there are 10 species of baleen whale. The largest is the blue whale – a rorqual and one of the biggest animals that has ever existed. In second place is the fin whale, another rorqual; unlike the blue whale, the fin usually travels in groups.

Sometimes 100 or more of these giants can be seen gathered together at good feeding grounds. The fin whale is an energetic swimmer, capable of speeds of over 40 km/h, nearly as fast as the sei whale, the fastest of the baleen whales, which reaches a maximum speed of 50km/h. Occasionally the fin breaches, making it the largest whale to do so as an adult, lifting its vast body – up to 24-27 m in length and 50-70 tonnes in weight – almost entirely clear of the water.

The third-biggest whale is the bowhead, the only baleen whale to live exclusively in Arctic waters and one of the few large creatures to remain there throughout the winter. Unlike fin and blue whales, which have a streamlined shape, the bowhead has a massive, bulky body. It rarely exceeds 18 m in length, but it can weigh up to 90 tonnes, the equivalent of 1200 men. The bowhead has the largest mouth of any whale and the longest baleen plates – those in the middle of its jaw may exceed 5 m. It lives alone or in small groups but often travels with smaller whales, particularly narwhals (meaning 'corpse' whales) and belugas (nicknamed sea canaries).

A close relative of the bowhead, and fourth in the giant stakes, is the right whale, so named because it was once considered the 'right' whale to kill. Unlike other whales, which sink after death, it floats at the surface, making it the favourite quarry of early commercial whalers, before the days of large factory ships. The right whale is also unusually easy to approach and often goes out of its way to investigate floating vessels. Playful and inquisitive, it sometimes nudges, pokes and even pushes objects along on the surface. It also performs 'headstands' with its tail in the air, using it like a sail to catch the

BREACHING HUMPBACKS Most baleen whales breach, leaping clear of the water. The exact purpose of this behaviour is not fully understood, although some scientists think it may be linked to breeding.

wind and drive itself slowly through the water. All of these attributes make the right whale popular with whale watchers. There are two races of right whale, the northern and the southern, in the Northern and Southern Hemispheres. They are sometimes categorised as two separate species.

Sadly, the right whale remains one of the most endangered whale species, despite the fact that it has been protected from hunting since 1937. Even by whale standards, it is an extremely slow breeder: females have their first calves at between 6 and 12 years of age and give birth once every three or four years.

Minke and pygmy right whales

Not all baleen whales are giants. Two species, minke whales and pygmy right whales, are comparatively small. Minke whales average around 8.5 m long as adults and are the most common of all baleen whales. They occur in almost all of the world's ocean waters and may even enter estuaries to feed. They were named after an infamous 18th-century Norwegian whaler, who constantly flouted the rules then governing the minimum size, and therefore species, of whales that could be caught.

Today, Norwegian vessels still hunt the minke, even though it has been protected by international law since 1986. The whalers argue that because of its abundance, their limited catch does not endanger the species, and as long as they do not trade the meat with other countries there is nothing to stop them. In 1993, however, a shipment of whale meat labelled 'shrimp' and destined for Asia was seized at Oslo airport. Japan remains the world's biggest consumer of

WHALE MIGRATION The grey whale, a medium-sized baleen whale that is found in the Pacific, makes the longest migration of any mammal, travelling 20 000 km each year between their summer feeding areas in the Arctic and their winter breeding zones off the west coast of Mexico. Blue whales, humpback whales and right whales make similar, but shorter journeys – southern right whales travel between Antarctica and the coasts of Africa, South America, Australia and New Zealand. Because the seasons are opposite in the Northern and Southern Hemispheres, whales from these two halves of the globe rarely meet.

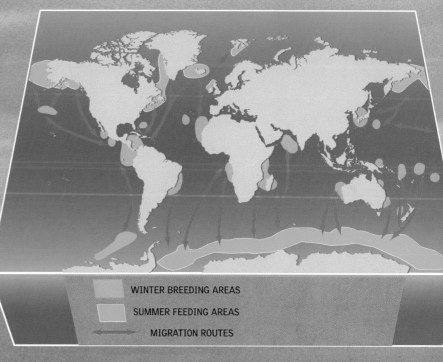

WINTER BREEDING AREAS
SUMMER FEEDING AREAS
MIGRATION ROUTES

whale meat. Officially, this meat all comes from dolphins and small whales caught in Japanese waters, but conservationists fear there may be an illegal trade supplying demand.

The world's smallest baleen whales are the pygmy right whales. These are far less common than minkes and occur only in temperate waters of the Southern Hemisphere. As adults, they rarely exceed 6.5 m long and weigh around 3 tonnes, the same as a large hippopotamus. The relatively small size and scarcity of pygmy right whales mean that they are rarely seen in the wild and little is known about their behaviour.

Humpback whales

Far more extensively studied is the humpback whale, a medium-sized baleen whale that attains a length of about 15 m and weighs up to 30 tonnes. Although named for the shape of its back when diving, it is best distinguished by its pectoral fins, or flippers. These are the longest of any animal on Earth: at around 4.5 m, they are nearly twice as long as those of any other whale. Humpback whales use their pectoral fins as paddles to help them change direction in the water. They also use them to stun prey – and possibly for communication – by slapping them against the water's surface.

Humpback whales are perhaps the most energetic of all baleen whales, frequently breaching, particularly in their breeding grounds. They also spy-hop, lifting their heads into the air to look around, and lobtail, slapping their huge tail flukes hard against the water. Like right whales, they are inquisitive and often approach boats. Each humpback whale has uniquely

FEEDING PARTY Humpback whales encircle fish with a 'net' of bubbles, driving a shoal tighter together. Several then burst up through the bubble net with their mouths wide open.

shaped and patterned tail flukes. This partly explains why the species has been so well studied, since it is easy for researchers to identify individual animals. Humpbacks are also more accessible than most other whales because they spend much of their time close to land and have fixed breeding grounds.

Long-term studies have revealed some fascinating findings. Humpback whales make massive migrations, swimming thousands of kilometres every year. They spend the summer in rich feeding grounds in cold seas, eating enough to build up thick reserves of blubber. In autumn they travel to warmer, less productive waters, where they breed and may go for months without feeding. They spend the winter in warmer waters for the sake of their calves. Scientists think higher temperatures allow newborn whales to channel more energy into growth, rather than wasting it in keeping warm.

Whale song

Most whales and dolphins produce a range of sounds, but male humpbacks sing long, loud and extremely complex songs. These are thought to be linked to breeding, advertising a male's fitness as a potential mate and warning other males to keep their distance. All the males in a particular population sing the same song (which typically lasts from 10 to 20 minutes), but the songs of geographically separated populations are different.

WHEN A BLUE WHALE IS BORN IT ALREADY WEIGHS MORE THAN 30 MEN AND IS LONGER THAN A GIRAFFE IS TALL. BY ADULTHOOD, A FULLY GROWN BLUE WHALE CAN WEIGH 200 TONNES, THE EQUIVALENT OF 14 LONDON BUSES, AND MEASURE 33.5 M FROM NOSE TO TAIL. Some of its blood vessels are big enough for a person to swim through. Its heart is the size of a family car. It is the largest creature known to have lived on Earth.

The blue whale maintains its massive bulk by feeding almost entirely on shrimplike krill – creatures no larger than a human finger. In order to build up the blubber on which it survives in the breeding season, the blue whale must eat around 4 tonnes of krill every day. It feeds by swimming through swarms of krill with its mouth open, then snapping its jaws shut. It squeezes out the water by pressing the krill against its baleen plates with a tongue that weighs as much as an elephant.

The blue whale's size made it a great prize in the days of whaling and, despite protection since 1967, its numbers remain low. Current estimates put the world population at around 3000 animals, just 1 per cent of what it was before whaling began on a large scale after 1900. In much of its virtually global range, the blue whale has yet to show signs of recovery. Only one population, in the north-east Pacific, has seen numbers grow by a significant amount.

The pygmy blue whale, a more compact version of the blue whale, lives in the Southern Hemisphere, mainly in the Indian Ocean. Unlike other blue whales, it stays in temperate waters all year round. Pygmy blue whales may be smaller than their cousins, but they are still enormous, reaching up to 22 m long.

BLUE WHALE

LIFE IN THE OPEN OC

EAN 6

MORE THAN HALF THE SURFACE OF THE PLANET IS OPEN OCEAN, a vast, featureless wilderness of water that stretches away in every direction. The ancient Greeks believed the ocean was endless, circling the land and continuing into infinity. In some respects, they were right: open ocean does encircle the Earth and could be travelled for an eternity without hitting land. These open waters may appear barren, but they are home to a dazzling variety of life. Animals are more scattered than on the ocean floor or around coastlines, but they are numerous and, like these short-nosed spinner dolphins, sometimes gather in large groups.

OCEAN DRIFTERS

SWIMMING IS OF LIMITED VALUE TO MANY OCEAN-DWELLERS. Although some creatures swim to catch prey and others swim to escape, many open-ocean animals survive perfectly well with only limited powers of movement. The oceans are filled with a multitude of drifting animals, from microscopic plankton to floating molluscs, who may travel thousands of miles carried along by the surface currents. In some places drifters form thick clouds; in others they are widely scattered. Many live by filtering out microscopic food particles from the water itself. Others pick off larger prey when it happens to come within reach.

Even many open-ocean predators are weak swimmers. Jellyfish, for example, can do little more than maintain their position in the water by pulsating their bell-shaped bodies. They travel almost entirely at the mercy of the currents, yet they survive in incredible numbers, catching whatever strays into their

JELLY STREAMS Salps filter water through their gelatinous bodies as they drift, retaining any food in it such as planktonic animals (visible top right).

trailing tentacles. The Portuguese man-o-war is another drifter that catches prey with stinging tentacles, but cannot travel by its own body movements at all. The man-o-war is not a single creature but a community of animals that live as a single unit, forming a 'creature' that can be up to 20 m long. One member of the colony forms an air-filled sac that floats on the surface with a 'sail' for catching the wind. Other members make up the tentacles, reproductive and digestive systems.

Other ocean drifters may appear even more weird to our land-bound senses. Salps are open-ocean cousins of sea squirts and live in a similar way, filtering food from the water. Although they do not look like it, salps are close relatives of vertebrates. Some live singly, drifting along like small, open-ended barrels of jelly; others form great chains that spiral or stretch out in the sea's surface waters. Salps can reproduce asexually, budding off new individuals that add themselves to the chain. They are also hermaphrodites so can reproduce sexually with any other member of the species that they meet.

Some drifters, such as the sea slug *Glaucus*, cling to the ocean surface, their bodies sticking to the underside of the meniscus – the curved surface that forms where water meets air. *Glaucus* increases its buoyancy by swallowing air, and sticking out from its sides are six winglike projections. Each one ends in a feather-like 'finger' filled with stinging cells that the slug takes from its prey, the Portuguese man-o-war, for protection. As the cells that *Glaucus* harvests are concentrated together, it is even more dangerous to humans than its infamous prey.

IN A PAPER-THIN SHELL

HANGING UPSIDE DOWN FROM A FROTHY RAFT OF BUBBLES, THE BUBBLE-RAFT SNAIL LOOKS A PICTURE OF DELICACY AND HELPLESSNESS AS IT FLOATS ON THE SURFACE OF THE OCEAN.

But appearances can be deceptive. It is a floating carnivore that devours any suitable victim it happens to bump into. It feeds on animals, such as stinging jellyfish and the deadly Portuguese man-o-war, that most other creatures avoid.

The bubble-raft snail inhabits tropical and subtropical waters. Unable to swim, it secretes a stream of mucus-covered bubbles from its foot, and this quickly hardens to provide a tiny vessel strong enough to carry the snail across the high seas. It travels entirely at the mercy of the winds and currents, relying on chance to drive it towards its prey. When it collides with a victim, it crawls partway onto it and feeds by rasping at it with a muscular, tonguelike organ known as a radula. This is covered with numerous tiny 'teeth', which give it a texture like sandpaper. A bubble-raft snail may remain attached to its prey for days or even weeks, disengaging only if the victim starts to sink. It is not immune to predators itself, but is counter-shaded to avoid detection (see page 113); as it hangs upside down, it is actually the top of its shell that is pale and the underside dark.

After mating, most molluscs lay their eggs and leave them to their fate. Bubble-raft snails take a little more care to help their offspring survive. Some brood their young and release them into the ocean as tiny, fully formed adults. Others set their eggs adrift attached to little rafts of their own: when the eggs hatch, the young remain clinging to their life raft until they are big enough to make rafts for themselves. All bubble-raft snails start life as males and transform into females as they grow older.

Bubble-raft snails cannot control where they go. Many end up in temperate waters, where they cannot survive. Before this, though, they may have travelled hundreds or even thousands of kilometres. Many wash up on North American and British shores, having been caught up by the Gulf Stream.

BUBBLE-RAFT SNAIL

NATURE'S POWERS

FOLLOWING THE CROWD

THE GREAT CLOUDS OF PLANKTON DRIFTING THROUGH THE OCEANS PROVIDE FOOD FOR SOME OF THE OCEANS' LARGEST INHABITANTS. Many of these follow currents, where plankton and other drifting animals become concentrated. Some make migrations to certain places at particular times of the year to take advantage of breeding swarms and other gatherings of prey. Every March, for example, whale sharks appear near Ningaloo Reef off Western Australia. These huge filter feeders remain in the area until July, when they head back out into the Indian Ocean. The arrival of the whale sharks at Ningaloo coincides with the massed spawning of the reef's corals. The sharks return every year to feed on the thick soup of eggs and sperm released into the water, and stay after the event to eat the planktonic coral larvae. Once the larvae have settled to become coral polyps and the bloom of other zooplankton that feed on them has subsided, the whale sharks head off for more productive waters elsewhere.

Giant appetites, tiny prey

The whale shark lives in tropical and subtropical waters. In the neighbouring temperate range, another giant lives and feeds in a similar way. At up to 12 m long and weighing 7 tonnes, the basking shark is the biggest fish found in temperate seas. It eats the same diet of plankton as the whale shark, but the two species are only distantly related. Both feed by swimming through clouds of plankton with their mouths open. They have bristle-like structures, known as gill rakers, stretched across the inside

BIG MOUTH The gape of a basking shark can measure more than 1 m across. As water flows through the shark's mouth, 10 cm-long gill rakers sift out tiny creatures, such as small crustaceans, fish eggs and larvae. The water is expelled through five pairs of gill slits that almost encircle the head. This individual was photographed off the coast of England.

FREE RIDE A remora clings to one of the fins on the side of a manta ray's head (right). The ray uses these fins to direct plankton-loaded water into its mouth. Remoras feed on scraps of food that get stuck around the ray's mouth, and hold onto their hosts using their dorsal fin, which has evolved into a suction cup.

As water passes through the gills, the rakers strain tiny creatures from the water. A basking shark can seive up to 2000 tonnes of water an hour.

openings of their gill slits. As water passes through the gills, these rakers strain tiny creatures from the water. A basking shark can seive up to 2000 tonnes of water an hour.

Like whale sharks, many basking sharks migrate seasonally to take advantage of plankton blooms. In summer, they start arriving off the west coast of Scotland when plankton concentrations are at their highest. As autumn begins, they travel down through the Irish Sea, then disperse into deeper water for the winter. In the western Atlantic, basking sharks appear in spring off the US coast from North Carolina to New York. They gradually make their way northwards, following plankton blooms, until they reach the waters off New England and Canada where they spend the summer. As winter approaches, they too disappear out into deeper water.

As the whale shark and basking shark illustrate, there is enough plankton in the open ocean to satisfy even the biggest appetites. One other giant that lives solely on plankton is the manta ray, the largest of the ray species. Unlike most rays, which spend much of their time on the bottom, manta rays swim continuously through open water. They move through the sea like gigantic, graceful birds, gently flapping their huge pectoral fins up and down like wings.

Manta rays live only in tropical and subtropical waters, concentrated around upwelling currents, where plankton tends to be richest. They feed by swimming with their mouths open wide, directing the flow of water inwards with the aid of flexible fins that extend from the head. Sometimes they perform loop-the-loops in the richest columns of upwelling water. Like the filter-feeding sharks, manta rays have structures on the insides of their gill slits that sift out food.

Group migrations

Many smaller open-ocean fish also feed on plankton. What they lack in size, they often make up for in numbers, forming shoals so dense and vast that they can block out the sunlight filtering down through the water. Mackerel, herrings and pilchards are all plankton-feeders that live in huge concentrations throughout the world's oceans. The movements of these fish are often directed by plankton blooms, and as a consequence, so are those of the creatures that feed on them.

One of the most spectacular and well-documented examples of this is the annual migration of pilchards along the South African coast. Around June and July, thick shoals of these fish numbering in their millions head towards the eastern coast of South Africa from farther out to sea. They are drawn by the northerly movement of cold, upwelling water that occurs at that time of year, and the subsequent appearance of the clouds of plankton on which they feed. In turn, the enormous pilchard shoals attract huge numbers of predators, including an estimated 23 000 dolphins and 100 000 cape gannets. Sharks and other large fish also arrive, and even ocean-going whales are drawn to the bonanza. At the height of the run, large shoals often come very close to the shore and pilchards can be netted from the beaches.

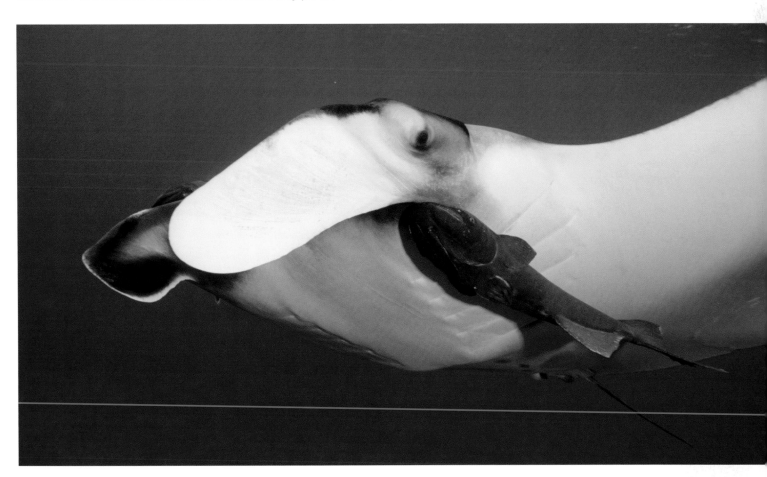

SAFETY IN NUMBERS

IN THE OPEN OCEAN THERE IS NOWHERE TO HIDE, SO OCEAN-DWELLERS HAVE COME UP WITH A VARIETY OF WAYS TO AVOID PREDATORS. Some, such as the miniature specks that collectively make up plankton, escape detection by virtue of their tiny size; others are transparent. Many achieve invisibility through a form of camouflage known as counter-shading. Still others protect themselves by crowding together in vast shoals to reduce their chances of falling victim to predators.

Chain reaction

Shoaling works because predators have difficulty picking off individual prey. A lone fish in open water may be easy to follow and catch, but when part of a group it becomes lost among other bodies. By moving as a mass, fish confuse the predator and offer each other cover. The urge to stay together is very strong in shoaling species. If an individual or small group becomes separated, its immediate instinct is to rejoin the larger mass. The bigger the shoal, the more bodies can hide within it – only those at the edges are really vulnerable.

If the shoal comes under attack, the fish within it bunch closer together and appear to move as a single unit. Although this movement may look complex from the outside, with fish making sudden, apparently simultaneous changes in direction, the mechanism behind it is quite simple. Rather than all following the same subtle cues, or communicating with each other in some way, fish within a shoal mimic the movements of the individuals in front of them. The time it takes for each fish to respond to its neighbour's moves is so short,

they create the illusion of all changing direction at once. The actual mechanism only becomes clear when watching film of a shoal in slow-motion.

Many open-water shoaling fish have silvery scales. These provide camouflage by scattering light, making the fish harder to detect in open water. If they are detected, the silvery scales take on a secondary role. Light reflected from one fish is almost equally reflected by the fish behind. This blurs their bodies together, making an individual much harder to pick out. Some species use other methods to blend in with the crowd. Mackerel, for instance, have silvery lower bodies and striped upper bodies. Seen from above, these stripes work in a similar way to those of herding zebras, breaking up individual outlines so the shoal appears like a single, large mass.

Hundreds of heads better than one

Shoaling evolved as a means of defence against predators, but recent research suggests that it may have a secondary function of improving direction-finding during migration and journeys to and from feeding sites. Researchers have long theorised that the direction or route taken by a shoal travelling to a fixed destination should be more accurate than that taken by an individual fish. Now there is evidence to back this up. Information taken from tagged coho salmon in the north-eastern Pacific shows that larger groups travel more directly and accurately

through the open ocean to their spawning rivers than smaller groups. Similar results have come from recent studies of migrating herrings. Life in a shoal, then, not only reduces a fish's chances of being caught by predators, but also improves its energy efficiency when travelling and increases its effectiveness in locating patches of planktonic food.

Mass food supply and oxygen generator

Some areas of the sea can support huge shoals of fish because of the presence of massive quantities of microscopic algae and other photosynthesising organisms, collectively known as phytoplankton, that live in the ocean's surface waters and form the base of the open-ocean food chain. Phytoplankton captures the Sun's energy to produce carbohydrates by photosynthesis, generating oxygen as a by-product. About half of all the oxygen in the Earth's atmosphere comes from phytoplankton, making it vital to life on land as well as in the sea.

The distribution of phytoplankton reflects the varying amounts of nutrients that occur in different parts of the sea. The most productive waters are fed by upwelling currents, which bring

minerals and other nutrients up from the sea bottom. Upwelling currents are common along the edges of continental shelves, the thick sections of the Earth's crust that project out around the major landmasses like raised underwater foundations. It also grows in some density over the continental shelves themselves. Because the sea is shallower here, there is more mixing between the bottom and surface waters, and more nutrients are brought up. Beyond the continental shelves, the Earth's crust is much thinner and the oceans are consequently deeper. Here, upwelling currents are common only around volcanic islands and seamounts that peak close to the surface.

Phytoplankton also grows profusely in large areas of open ocean where upwelling water is drawn out to sea by surface currents. One such band stretches out from Ecuador into the Pacific Ocean; another points like a finger south-eastwards from the Horn of Africa.

PART OF THE IN-CROWD Flat-iron herring gather in dense shoals off Mexico's Pacific coast. They are preyed upon by a number of species, including the leopard grouper.

COUNTER-SHADING
Many open-ocean residents, from large sharks to tiny fish, are a darker shade or colour on top and lighter underneath. Long-jawed mackerel (right), for example, are blue-green on top with silvery undersides. Being darker on top helps fish to blend in with the blue of the ocean when seen from above, protecting them from diving birds, while pale undersides make them harder to spot from below, against the light flooding down from above. Some creatures that inhabit deep water even make their own light to fool would-be predators. The hatchetfish, for instance, has rows of light-producing organs on its belly. These generate a pale blue light that closely matches light penetrating from the surface. Hatchetfish can regulate the exact colour and intensity of the light they produce, enabling them to remain invisible as they move up or down through the water column.

OUT OF THE BLUE

FOR THE HUNTER, THE OPEN OCEAN IS LIKE A DESERT DOTTED WITH OASES. Vast areas are almost devoid of prey fish and other large animals, but here and there are dense schools of fish, drawn by blooms of plankton. Predators, whether hunting alone or in shoals, may go for days without a meal. They cannot afford to risk missing any chances of food, so have developed extreme speed, finely tuned senses of hearing, taste and sight, and well-honed tactics to locate and catch prey. Many are drawn by sounds or vibrations caused by other predators on the attack. Rarely is one species able to feed alone on prey it has found.

Open-water hunters are strong and swift – at least over short distances – and include the fastest swimmers in the sea. Marlin and their close relatives, the sailfish, for example, can reach over 100 km/h in short bursts. The bluefin tuna, swordfish, spotted dolphin and Dall's porpoise are all known for their speed. Even some sharks living in open water are built for speed rather than power. The shortfin mako shark, for instance, is shaped like a flattened bullet, with a conical snout and slender, muscular body. It feeds on tuna and other fast-moving fish, and is capable of over 95 km/h in short bursts, making it the fastest of all sharks. Its counter-shading and streamlined shape has earned it the common name of mackerel shark. Mako is not a corruption of mackerel, but a Maori word for shark that was later applied to this species.

Cooperative hunting

Not all open-water predators rely on speed alone to catch prey. Some also employ cooperative behaviour and other tools. Several species of dolphin inhabit the ocean's wide-open spaces and all of them live and hunt in groups. Dolphins find their prey using echolocation, sending out bursts of clicks, then listening for any echoes that may bounce back. Echolocation enables them to scour the open ocean and detect prey that may be quite distant. It also gives them an idea of how far away prey is – the longer it takes for echoes to return, the farther off are the objects from which they were reflected. A hunting pod of dolphins often spreads out to form a wide front, increasing the chances of one of its members finding prey. If prey is located, the rest of the pod is notified by whistles and the hunt begins.

When hunting schooling fish, dolphins in a pod work together. If the school is large, they try to force a small portion to break away. This is easier said than done, as instinct drives the fish to rejoin the main school. In the end persistent pressure usually succeeds in separating off some of the fish. These then gather together in a smaller school, known as a bait ball. The dolphins keep the bait ball together by circling it and try to drive it up to the surface. There are two reasons why they do this: the surface itself acts as a barrier, helping to pen the fish in, and the dolphins themselves need to be near the surface to breathe. If the bait ball escapes into deeper water, the dolphins may lose it altogether. With the bait ball trapped near the surface, the dolphins take turns to swim through it and snap up fish. The commotion at the surface often attracts seabirds, which dive into the bait ball from above. Other predators are attracted by the sound of the dolphins' sonar or by vibrations in the water. Sharks arrive drawn by the scent of blood, although many are also attracted by sound.

Power players

The mako shark is well adapted to the open ocean because its circulation system functions like that of warm-blooded creatures, giving it the energy for bursts of speed. Many other shark species live in the open ocean too, feeding on squid and fish. The blue shark inhabits almost all of the world's tropical and temperate seas, hunting from the surface to depths of around 350 m. Like the mako, the blue shark has a long, pointed snout and is highly streamlined, but its body is less flattened vertically and its pectoral fins are much longer. It can also achieve fast speeds. The blue shark feeds on similar prey to the mako but is more opportunistic, using its sense of smell and large eyes to home in on prey captured by others. It is often the first shark to arrive at bait balls created by dolphins.

Thresher sharks are less speedy than either blue sharks or makos, but they are widespread and efficient open-ocean hunters. Thresher sharks are unique in having a tail fin that is longer than the rest of their body. For a long time the purpose of this fin was poorly understood, but recent observations have shed light on the mystery. Thresher sharks have been seen using their whiplike tails to herd and then stun prey near the surface. Such sightings have been backed up by catches from long-line fishing vessels. Many landed thresher sharks have been hooked by the tail rather than the mouth, which suggests that they were hitting bait fish dragging along on the lines in an attempt to disable them before feeding. Like blue sharks, threshers are found throughout the world's tropical and temperate seas. In fact, mako, blue and thresher sharks have ranges that overlap. However, unlike blue and mako sharks,

FOOD FOR ALL Dolphins work together to herd shoals of fish. They circle beneath their prey to drive them towards the surface (above). Then they take turns to dart through the mass of bodies to snap up a meal. Dolphins use the surface as a barrier to prevent fish escaping, and this technique brings their prey within reach of other predators. Seabirds are quick to spot feeding dolphins and dive into the shoals from above (right). Other predators are often drawn by the activity, including sharks, marlin and tuna.

SAILFISH

VITAL STATISTICS

COMMON NAMES: Cosmopolitan sailfish, bayonet fish, peacock fish
LATIN NAME: *Istiophorus platypterus*
MAXIMUM LENGTH: 3.4 m
MAXIMUM WEIGHT: 100 kg
TOP SPEED: 109 km/h
HABITAT: Open ocean
DIET: Fish and squid

THE FASTEST SWIMMER ON EARTH,

THIS SUPER-STREAMLINED PREDATOR CAN REACH SPEEDS OF 109 KM/H OVER SHORT DISTANCES AS IT CUTS THROUGH THE WATER TO SNAP UP PREY. Cosmopolitan sailfish spend their lives in the open ocean, cruising near the surface in a constant search for food, sometimes with the dorsal fin, which can be twice as high as the body is deep, projecting above the surface. They only turn on the speed when they sight prey, powering in to catch it before it disappears into the blue.

Cosmopolitan sailfish hunt mainly in surface waters and use vision to locate prey. Their prey varies in different parts of their range, which includes all of the world's tropical and temperate seas. In the Atlantic, sailfish catch mainly mackerel, small tuna, jack and needlefish, while in the Indian and Pacific Oceans they more commonly catch sardines, anchovies and ribbonfish. They sometimes eat squid. Their prey are mainly fast-moving, agile species, but all are significantly smaller than the sailfish – and none can move fast enough to escape it.

When a sailfish discovers prey, it begins by chasing the shoal at half speed, slowly closing the distance between them. Once within range, it surges in suddenly for the attack, swiping its swordlike bill through the school to stun or kill individuals before snapping them up.

Sometimes it may bunch prey fish together before attacking, overtaking a shoal and then turning and opening out its sail to startle them. Adult cosmopolitan sailfish often travel alone, but sometimes they gather and hunt in small groups, apparently working together to corral prey, and using their dorsal fins to form a barrier so the fish cannot escape.

In some areas, cosmopolitan sailfish undertake annual migrations, following their food as it, in turn, follows seasonal blooms of plankton. In the East China Sea, cosmopolitan sailfish travel north in summer, then south as autumn sets in. In the Indian Ocean, they gather off the African coast around the time of the monsoon rains, when the East African Coastal Current becomes most productive, boosted by nutrients washed off the land.

which live largely solitary lives, threshers often travel and hunt in small, loose groups whose size depends on the quantity of food in the area.

Speed and surprise

After sharks, perhaps the open-ocean predators most feared by humans are the barracudas. This reputation is largely undeserved, as these fish almost never attack unprovoked. When they do, it is usually a case of mistaken identity – jewellery or other shiny objects being taken for the flashing scales of fish. Barracudas inhabit the surface waters of tropical and subtropical oceans. There are 18 species and all have a similarly intimidating appearance. With their underslung jaws and long bodies they have a superficial resemblance to pike, but unlike those freshwater ambushers, barracudas are fast-moving, active predators that hunt by daylight and locate prey primarily by sight. They rely on surprise and quick bursts of speed to catch their victims.

Barracudas are large: the biggest, the great barracuda, can reach 1.8 m long and 50 kg in weight and attain speeds of up to 58 km/h. Most live in shoals and hunt other schooling fish, such as snappers, small tuna, mullet and herring, charging in with frightening speed to grab their prey. Their long jaws give them a wide gape, which allows them to tackle quite large prey, and their two sets of razor-sharp teeth can easily tear through flesh. Smaller fish are swallowed whole, while larger fish have chunks torn off them or are bitten in half by the barracuda's formidable teeth.

Giant tuna

Despite their large size and fearsome appearance, barracudas can and do fall prey to other fish. Among the fish that hunt smaller adult barracuda are the larger species of tuna, such as the bluefin. Bluefin tuna are truly massive, growing to lengths of 4.5 m and weighing up to 650 kg – as much as nine men. These giants live in shoals and are high-speed hunters, capable of reaching 88 km/h in short bursts as they charge after prey. The bluefin tuna is one of the world's largest bony fish (some sharks are bigger, but they have skeletons made of cartilage) and outside polar waters it has an almost global range. However, years of pressure from both commercial and sport fishermen have virtually wiped out the bluefin in many areas.

Yellowfin tuna are smaller than bluefins but still massive fish. They can grow to around 2.4 m long and weigh 200 kg. Yellowfins are far more common than their larger cousins and form massive shoals in the open oceans of the tropics and subtropical regions. As with bluefins, yellowfins of a particular size and age tend to stick together, with the largest individuals forming shoals of their own. Big yellowfin tuna are often found

SHAPED FOR SPEED Bluefin tuna are massive, streamlined hunters that cruise the open ocean in search of prey. Their great size and delicious meat have made them a prime target for fishermen over the years and they are now endangered across much of their range.

in association with dolphins. It is thought that they follow the marine mammals, which are better at finding prey. Fishermen have long known about this association and use the appearance of dolphins at the surface to lead them to tuna shoals.

Escape strategies

With so many large, fast-moving predators in the open ocean, it is a challenge for small fish to survive at all. Most opt for camouflage and safety in numbers, confusing and escaping predators through their sheer massed abundance. A few species use less conventional methods to escape being eaten. Flying fish escape predators by taking to the air. Their pectoral fins are so long and broad they can act as wings, catching the updrafts from waves and carrying the fish as much as 200 m over the surface. In water, flying fish hold their fins close against the sides of their bodies to minimise friction and only open them at the moment they leap into the air.

Other fish seek protection in unlikely places. Young golden trevally live among the tentacles of jellyfish and Portuguese men-o-war; they are covered with a mucus that neutralises the poison from their hosts' stinging cells. As they grow larger, the trevallies leave the protection of their invertebrate hosts and seek out bigger allies, such as whale sharks and manta rays. Adult golden trevallies are sometimes called pilot fish for their habit of swimming in the bow waves that form just in front of these huge creatures. As well as getting a free ride, the trevally gains a measure of protection from its massive travelling companion, which intimidates most predators and also partially shields the trevally from view.

MARVELS OF THE SEA

MEDIAEVAL MAPS SHOW THE OPEN OCEAN POPULATED BY HUGE MONSTERS. Early mariners brought back tales of incredible creatures and cartographers incorporated many of them into their maps. Some were pure fantasy, combining the features of land animals with the bodies of fish; others really existed. One of the most terrifying sea monsters of legend was the kraken, which had roots in Norse mythology where it appeared in various forms. The shape that passed into modern art and literature, through late 18th-century accounts, was that of a gigantic octopus or squid so large it could attack ships, its tentacles reaching out of the water and onto the decks.

Tales of the kraken are now thought to have been inspired by encounters with giant squid. In 2003, French sailors described the experience of a giant squid attaching itself to the hull of their yacht (see page 97), echoing stories related by mariners centuries earlier. The giant squid is the world's largest-known living invertebrate – from the tip of its nose cone to the end of its tentacles it may be 18 m long and can weigh up to 2 tonnes. It is certainly big enough to strike fear into the heart of the hardiest sailor and to be regarded as a monster by those on land.

Colossus of the deep

Although the giant squid is the probable source of the kraken legend, another creature from the deep attains a similar size – the colossal squid, which lives in Antarctic waters. Until recently, the colossal squid was even less known than the giant squid, mainly because of the inhospitableness of the seas it inhabits. In 2003, however, a virtually complete juvenile specimen was retrieved from the Ross Sea in the Southern Ocean. Although parts of its tentacles had been lost, its nose cone, or mantle, measured 2.5 m long. Based on this, scientists estimate that adults grow to 4 m in mantle length. Unlike the giant squid, which has a ring of sharp teeth around each of its suckers, the colossal squid is armed with swivelling hooks on its longest tentacles for grappling prey. This enables it to tackle large fish such as the Patagonian toothfish, which grows to more than 2 m long, and other open-water

STING IN THE TAIL Two southern stingrays drift slowly over the sandy seabed off the Cayman Islands. Rays are most closely related to sharks and like them have skeletons made of cartilage rather than bone. Stingrays have a venomous spine on their tails, which they use to defend themselves if attacked.

SEA SERPENT The oarfish is a likely source of stories about sea serpents. Its pectoral fins pivot as it swims, like the oars of a rowing boat.

sea creatures, killing them with a venomous bite from its massive, parrot-like beak. Despite being such a formidable and aggressive predator, it is itself, like the giant squid, hunted by sperm whales.

Giant serpents

Sailors used the term sea serpent for many of the creatures that they came across. Some true snakes do inhabit the oceans, spending their entire lives in the water. Most give birth to live young at sea, making them the only reptiles to have completely divorced themselves from the land. These sea snakes move like eels and have flat tails to drive themselves through the water. Most are highly venomous, and all can dislocate their jaws as land snakes can, enabling them to swallow fish whole.

However, sea snakes are relatively small – the largest species grows to a maximum length of 2.7 m – and although they are common in tropical waters, they were probably not the sea serpents of myth. A more likely contender for this title is the harmless oarfish, a creature which can grow up to 8 m long, and there are unconfirmed reports of even larger individuals. As its name suggests, the oarfish has a long, flattened body. It has a wide distribution, including the North Sea and open Atlantic. It normally lives at depths of 200-1000 m, but occasionally swims near the surface and is sometimes washed up on beaches. Given its length, it is not hard to imagine it becoming the inspiration for legends.

Baskers and bottom-dwellers

Not all of the world's giant fish have inspired legends. The sunfish never made it into myth or onto maps. This enormous creature slowly cruises the open ocean in search of jellyfish. Sometimes it basks at the surface, lying on its side with the other side of its flattened body facing the sky, hence its name. The sunfish uses its dorsal and anal fins to move, but it is a relatively weak swimmer and often allows itself to be carried along by the currents. In the Atlantic Ocean it is sometimes transported, with its jellyfish prey, by the Gulf Stream and has been spotted off the British Isles.

The sunfish is the heaviest of the bony fishes. It frequently grows to weights in excess of a tonne, but as a hatchling it is tiny, measuring just 2.5 mm long. The largest adult sunfish may be 60 million times the size it was when its life began, the equivalent of a human baby growing to the weight of six *Titanic*s.

Many weird and wonderful creatures live on or near the seabed, including most types of ray, which spend their lives hunting the many smaller creatures there. Rays have flattened bodies and move using winglike pectoral fins. In most species, these fins merge so neatly with the rest of the body they appear to be extensions of it, rather than highly evolved appendages. Some rays flap their fins up and down, while others move by rippling their muscles. Apart from a few large plankton-eating species, such as the manta and devil rays, all are carnivores and have mouths positioned on their undersides.

FLATTENED PADDLER The sunfish can grow to more than 3 m long and around 1.5 tonnes. Like the much smaller triggerfish, which feeds on coral, it swims by undulating its dorsal (top) and anal (bottom) fins.

Most rays use their mouths to catch prey, but one group uses electricity. Torpedo rays, which occur in most of the world's tropical and temperate seas, hunt by sneaking up on other fish, wrapping their fins around them and delivering a powerful electric shock. Some species can produce jolts of up to 220 volts, more than enough to kill most of their prey outright. The electricity is generated by two kidney-shaped organs just behind the head. These are composed of stacks of specialised muscle with nerve endings concentrated on one side. When the muscles are contracted, an electrical charge builds up on that side and is released into the water as a shock.

FRUITS OF THE SEA
Fishermen on Ifaluk Atoll in the Caroline Islands, east of the Philippines, return with a catch of tuna. For many island peoples, fishing is a way of life and the sea a major source of food. Local waters are often known almost as intimately as the islands themselves, and the best spots for catching certain fish are common knowledge.

LIVING WITH THE SEA

The Bajo's name for themselves, *Sama dilau*, means 'people of the sea'. They fished to supply their own needs and in order to trade with land-based peoples. For centuries, the Bajo were the main suppliers of pearls in South-east Asia, and of sea cucumbers, which they dried out and sold as 'trepang' for use in cooking.

SEEN FROM SPACE, THE PACIFIC OCEAN is a vast expanse of blue dotted with tiny specks of land. For millions of years, those specks were inhabited only by plants and animals, cut off from the rest of the world by virtually endless tracts of open water. It was just 2000 years ago that the first people began to arrive. Unlike the plants and animals that colonised the islands before them, people came not by accident but by design, and brought everything with them that they might need in their new settlements, including livestock, food plants and seeds.

Natural signposts

The colonisation of the Pacific began with Samoa in the west. From there, voyagers headed eastwards, discovering and settling the Marquesas Islands in the centre of the Pacific. They then travelled northwards to Hawaii and farther east to Easter Island. Around 1000 years ago, they made the 6500 km journey from the Marquesas south-west to New Zealand. Although these people set off not knowing where or when their journeys might end, they had the skills to detect islands long before they could see them. They discovered new land using natural clues. High islands, for example, were known to create high clouds, which prevailing winds blew into trails across the sky like smoke signals. Lower islands were located by their effect on the ripples of the sea's surface, and could be detected even when still a long way over the horizon. Seabirds also helped the Pacific voyagers to locate new lands. Some species were known never to travel far from their nesting sites, so the voyagers followed birds that they spotted. In addition, they had an intimate knowledge of the stars, which they used to maintain their course at night.

Navigation and sailing skills were passed down through the generations and are still used by some Polynesians today. Collectively, they are known as 'way-finding'. Before the arrival of modern navigation equipment way-finding was vital, even for travel between neighbouring islands – in the Pacific, these could be dozens and sometimes hundreds of kilometres apart. Fishermen and other seafarers also built up a comprehensive knowledge of local currents and wave patterns to help them find their way home when their own islands had slipped beyond the horizon. In Micronesia, simple maps were made by lashing together sticks that showed the relative positions of islands and the directions of currents between them. These were not taken to sea but were used as tools for teaching apprentice navigators, who memorised the information and added to it as their experience increased.

Dependent on the sea

Life for most island peoples is intimately tied to the sea. Many still live in close harmony with the ocean, as they have done for centuries, relying on it to supply most of their needs. Subsistence fishing is still practised on many islands in Indonesia, the world's largest archipelago. One tribe there, the Bajo, even abandoned the land altogether: until the middle of the 20th century they were nomadic, living on houseboats and travelling between moorings. Today, most of the Bajo live in coastal villages or stilt-houses built on reefs in the sea.

The Bajo's name for themselves, *Sama dilau*, means 'people of the sea'. They fished to supply their own needs and in order to trade with land-based peoples. For centuries, the Bajo were the main suppliers of pearls in South-east Asia, and of sea cucumbers, which they dried out and sold as 'trepang' for use in cooking. They traded these luxuries for essentials that the sea could not provide, such as fresh water, firewood and vegetables. Although most of the Bajo are now settled, their links to the sea remain strong. Their stilt-house communities are built over shallow water to give them easy access to fishing. Many who live in these sea villages walk on stilts to get from one house to another. Naturally, they are skilled boat-builders and mariners, with detailed knowledge of local and more distant waters.

Marine industries

Living off the sea is not always about subsistence. Many people from Western nations rely on the oceans for employment and income. It is estimated that 16 per cent of all the protein eaten by humans comes from the sea. The UK alone has a fleet of more than 4000 fishing vessels – even after the cutbacks of recent years – all operating commercially to supply the population with seafood.

The international fishing industry is huge and employs millions of people, hundreds of thousands of whom crew the boats and haul in the catch. Those working on the larger factory ships may spend months at a time at sea. These vessels not only catch fish, but process and freeze it, only returning to port when they are full. As a result, crews spend most of their working lives away from land, in many ways living their own, modern version of the sea-going nomadic existence.

Sailors spend long periods at sea, and their jobs are vital to modern lifestyles. Most imported cars are transported by sea, as are the majority of imported electrical goods and other household items. Oil, the very lifeblood of developed economies, is moved by mariners. The world's largest ships are oil tankers: the biggest of all, the *Jahre Viking*, is an incredible 458.5 m from bow to stern, long enough to carry the Eiffel Tower laid on its side with room for half a Tower to spare.

CEREMONIAL CATCH A Moken diver takes a turtle from the Andaman Sea for a wedding ritual. To the Moken people, to harpoon a turtle is to marry a woman. Many island cultures are deeply connected to the ocean and attribute ritual significance to numerous marine creatures.

THE
OCEAN
DEPTHS

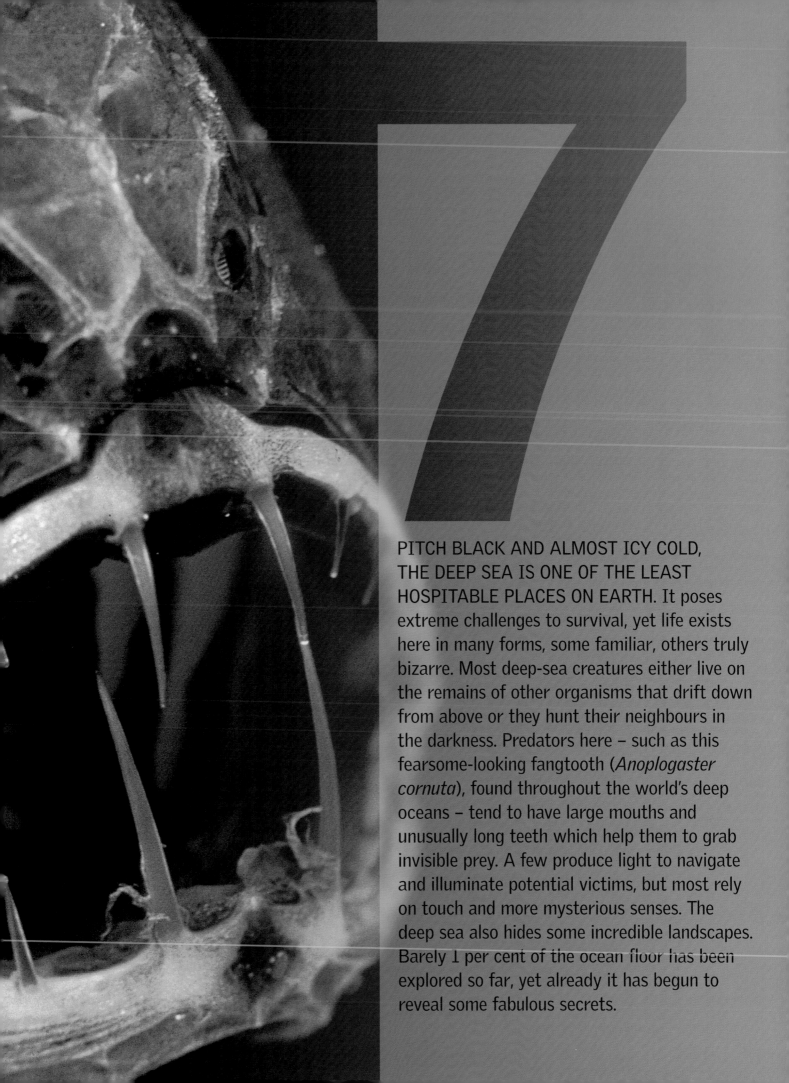

7

PITCH BLACK AND ALMOST ICY COLD, THE DEEP SEA IS ONE OF THE LEAST HOSPITABLE PLACES ON EARTH. It poses extreme challenges to survival, yet life exists here in many forms, some familiar, others truly bizarre. Most deep-sea creatures either live on the remains of other organisms that drift down from above or they hunt their neighbours in the darkness. Predators here – such as this fearsome-looking fangtooth (*Anoplogaster cornuta*), found throughout the world's deep oceans – tend to have large mouths and unusually long teeth which help them to grab invisible prey. A few produce light to navigate and illuminate potential victims, but most rely on touch and more mysterious senses. The deep sea also hides some incredible landscapes. Barely 1 per cent of the ocean floor has been explored so far, yet already it has begun to reveal some fabulous secrets.

PERILOUS DESCENT

EXPLORING THE DEEP SEA IS A RISKY BUSINESS. Every dive has an element of danger, and if anything goes wrong, the chances of rescue are slim. Because of the danger to human lives, all deep-sea dives are planned carefully down to the last detail. Many are undertaken by unmanned, remotely operated vessels.

One of the chief dangers involved in diving comes from changes in pressure: the deeper one goes, the greater the pressure becomes. Objects at the surface – at sea level – experience air pressure defined as one atmosphere (1 atm). But because water is much denser than air, the pressure of its weight increases much more rapidly with depth. At a depth of 10 m, the pressure is double that at the surface, or 2 atm. At 20 m it is 3 atm; at 30 m 4 atm, and so on.

Pressure and 'the bends'

Scuba and skin divers feel the effect of this increasing pressure mainly through their ears. As the pressure increases outside, the eardrum is pushed inward, causing pain – passengers on jet aeroplanes experience something similar as a plane depressurises before coming in to land. As divers descend, they try to 'equalise' the pressure: by holding their breath and pushing they can increase the air pressure behind the eardrum in order to cancel out the effect of the increasing pressure outside. Failure to equalise properly can result in permanent damage to the ear.

Returning to the surface can also cause problems if the ascent is too rapid. With increasing pressure, the volume of the lungs decreases while the density of the air inside them increases. Rapid ascent can cause the lungs to expand too quickly. Even more dangerous is the risk of developing decompression sickness, or 'the bends'. Under increased pressure, nitrogen from the air breathed in builds up in the body's tissues – unlike oxygen, nitrogen is not used up by the body. As a diver ascends and the pressure drops, the nitrogen re-enters the bloodstream and returns to the lungs. But if the ascent is too rapid, the nitrogen may be forced out of the body tissues as

GOING DOWN An unmanned submersible is gently lowered into the Black Sea from a research ship. Remotely operated vessels like this are increasingly being used to explore the deep sea, where intense pressure and uncharted terrain make it dangerous to dive or to go down in manned submarines.

gas bubbles. These can interfere with circulation and cause pain in the joints and muscles. In extreme cases, the bends can cause strokelike symptoms and divers can die unless treated. The bends are avoided by making 'decompression stops' on the way back up to the surface, and by limiting the number and frequency of dives in any one period.

The deeper a diver descends, the more extreme the effects of pressure become. Scuba divers rarely descend below around 100 m and the effects they experience can be dealt with relatively easily. At greater depths, however, the pressure can be too much for the human body. Deep-sea divers, such as those building and maintaining oil rigs, wear specially designed suits to protect them from harm. These may be either all-in-one jointed steel suits, which also protect them from the bends, or canvas and rubber suits with metal helmets, which do not. Divers wearing the latter gear either breathe a special combination of gases or make regular decompression stops on the way back up. Both types of suit are normally connected to the surface by a lifeline, used to haul the diver up.

Exploring with submersibles

Modern deep-sea diving suits are designed to operate safely at depths of up to 610 m. But beyond the continental shelf, the average depth of the seabed is around 3.6 km, and to explore these zones submersibles are needed. The first submersible capable of reaching such depths was the bathysphere (the name comes from the Greek *bathos*, meaning 'depth'), which was a spherical steel vessel designed and operated by two Americans, Charles William Beebe and Otis Barton. In 1934, they used a

bathysphere to reach a depth of 923 m – at the time, by far the deepest that anyone had ever been. But the bathysphere had limits. Although physically capable of surviving the pressure at great depths, it was lowered into and raised from the deep by a cable attached to a ship. If the cable snapped, there was no way of bringing the bathysphere back to the surface.

With this in mind, in 1947 the Swiss physicist Auguste Piccard built the world's first bathyscaphe, a self-propelled submarine designed to operate at extreme depths. Piccard took it down to 4000 m in 1954. By this time, he had already built his second bathyscaphe, *Trieste*, and in 1960 it set a world depth record of 10 920 m when his son Jacques copiloted it into the Mariana Trench. At the bottom of the trench, the *Trieste* withstood 364 atm of pressure, the equivalent of a 1.17 tonne weight being applied to every square centimetre of the vessel's surface. The bathyscaphe carried petrol for buoyancy and iron pellets for ballast. It descended by pumping water into air tanks at either end of its structure and rose by jettisoning the iron pellets and pumping the water out again.

Manned submersibles are still sometimes used, but today unmanned craft do much of the work. These are remotely operated from ships at the surface, and because they do not have to carry people, they are freer from size constraints. In 1985, a remotely operated submersible called *Argo* first located the wreck of the *Titanic*; later, a smaller robot called *Jason*, operated from a research submarine, explored the liner. In 2005, the British Submarine Escape and Rescue team used a remote-controlled Scorpio submersible to free the Russian minisub *Priz*, which had become entangled in a discarded fishing net on the seafloor off Siberia's Kamchatka peninsula. Armed with cutting pincers, the Scorpio, specially designed for submarine rescue, sliced through the netting which had held the *Priz* and its crew members captive for three days. All seven men on board the Russian submarine returned to the surface safely.

DEPTH ZONES

New worlds unfold as the ocean plunges to dark and chilly depths beyond the reach of sunlight. Scientists divide this underwater environment into two basic zones: the pelagic zone, the ocean itself; and the benthic zone, the ocean floor. They further subdivide the pelagic zone into the sunlit (or euphotic) zone at the top, the twilight (or dysphotic) zone and the midnight (or aphotic) zone.

AS DEPTH INCREASES, SO DOES

PRESSURE At 5 m the pressure is enough to cause pain in human eardrums: at 25 m it can make them burst. Considering the danger pressure poses to our bodies when we dive beneath the sea, it seems strange that fish and other creatures can survive in the deep ocean without suffering any ill effects. The reason they are able to do so is that the pressure within their bodies is equal to that of the water outside them. Rather than being crushed at depth, they expand if they are brought to the surface. Some deep-sea fish pulled up quickly have even been known to explode.

THE PRESSURE PARADOX

30 m

South Pacific divers have been known to gather pearls at depths of 50 m.

78 m

The deepest-ever constant-ballast dive by a woman. Canadian diver Mandy-Rae Cruickshank reached 78 m off the Cayman Islands in May 2004. In constant-ballast diving, the diver must descend and ascend on a single breath. She can carry weights to help her descend, but she must bring them back up to the surface again.

171 m

The deepest no limits free dive by a man, made by French diver Loïc Leferme off Villefranche, France, in October 2004.

100M

103 m

The deepest-ever constant-ballast dive by a man. Czech diver Martin Stepanek achieved this record in Greece in September 2004.

160 m

The deepest no-limits free dive by a woman, achieved by US diver Tanya Streeter off the Turks and Caicos Islands in August 2002. In no-limits freediving, the diver slides down a cable on a weighted sled, then uses air-assistance to get back to the surface, all in a single breath.

200M

270 m

The deepest point at which photosynthesis can occur – beyond about 270 m there are no seaweeds or living phytoplankton. The deepest photosynthesising organism discovered to date was a reef-forming red alga, found at 268 m.

318.25 m

The deepest-ever scuba dive, made by South African diver Nuno Gomes in the Red Sea in June 2005.

300M

385 m

The deepest unassisted seafloor walk. US oceanographer Sylvia Earle (left) used a pressurised suit to walk the ocean floor off

BEYOND HUMAN LIMITS

400M

480 m
The deepest successful underwater rescue. In 1973, the two-man crew of the submersible *Pisces III* were rescued off Ireland using a remotely controlled undersea recovery vessel.

500M

565 m
The greatest depth reached by the deepest-diving bird, the emperor penguin of the Antarctic.

600M

608 m
The maximum diving depth of nuclear-powered attack submarines.

700M

THE TWILIGHT ZONE

LIGHT SLOWLY FADES FROM THE OCEAN AS DEPTH INCREASES Just 200 m down it is already very faint – too faint for most seaweeds and phytoplankton to survive. From here to 1000 m is the so-called Twilight Zone, the area of the ocean that separates the sunlit surface from the darkness of the deep sea. Many of the creatures that live here are black or red, such as the gulper eel and this brittlestar, making them effectively invisible (red wavelengths do not reach this depth). Some, such as anglerfish, produce their own light to attract prey or others of their own kind. A few do so to camouflage themselves against the small amounts of light filtering down from the surface.

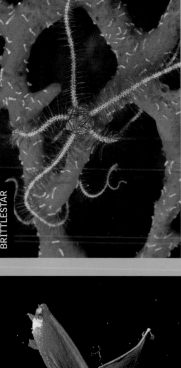
BRITTLESTAR

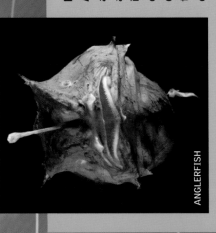
ANGLERFISH

GULPER EEL

800M

900M

DARKNESS

EVEN IN THE CLEAREST SEAS, NO LIGHT PENETRATES BELOW 1000 M

Everything is cold and dark, and pressures are immense. This is sometimes called the Midnight Zone. Its waters make up the vast majority of those in the ocean, the average ocean depth being 3837 m. The Midnight Zone of the ocean is effectively the world's largest natural habitat, yet we know almost nothing about it. Most of the creatures discovered here are known only from individuals brought up from the depths. Vast areas remain completely unexplored.

1000M

1215 m
The greatest depth reached by the deepest-diving reptile, the leatherback turtle.

2000M

1200 m
The maximum operating depth of *Deepstar 4000*, a manned research submersible.

1500 m
The maximum depth reached by the deepest-diving seal, the northern elephant seal.

1500 m
The depth of a giant squid photographed live off Japan's Bonin Islands. Giant squid also live at much greater depths.

3000M

3000 m
The greatest depth reached by the sperm whale, the deepest-diving animal.

2481 m
The depth of the first hydrothermal vents ever discovered, in 1977 at the Galápagos Rift.

3837 m
The average ocean depth.

3845 m
The depth of the *Titanic*. In 1987, the submersible *Nautile* was used to recover artefacts from the wreck; in 1998 it helped to salvage a piece of the hull wall.

4000M

4500 m
The maximum operating depth of the research submersible *Alvin*.

- **4050 m**
  The maximum operating depth of the remotely operated vehicle *Tiburon*.
- Depth of the first transatlantic cable, laid in August 1858. The 4000 km cable connected Ireland and Newfoundland, Canada.

4500 m
The deepest point in the Southern Ocean.

4759 m
The depth of the wreck of the World War II German warship, *Bismarck*.

5000M

5000 m
The deepest recorded octopus, the dumbo. It flaps its fins as it swims.

5450 m
The deepest point in the Arctic Ocean.

5639 m
The deepest recorded sponges –

DEEPSTAR 4000

GIANT SQUID

THE NAUTILE

DUMBO OCTOPUS

GLASS SPONGE

DEEPEST POINTS

6000M

6075 m
The deepest operating depth of the three-man Russian submersibles *Mir I* and *Mir II*.

7000M

7450 m
The deepest point in the Indian Ocean – the Java Trench.

8000M

8648 m
The deepest point in the Atlantic Ocean – the Puerto Rico Trench.

CUSK EEL

8372 m
The deepest recorded fish, a cusk eel.

9000M

9789 m
The deepest recorded invertebrate – a tiny shrimp-like amphipod crustacean.

AMPHIPOD

10 000M

10 920 m
The deepest point on Earth – the Mariana Trench in the Pacific Ocean – visited by Jacques Piccard and Donald Walsh in the bathyscaphe *Trieste* in 1958. It is inhabited by single-celled creatures called foraminifera and other simple organisms.

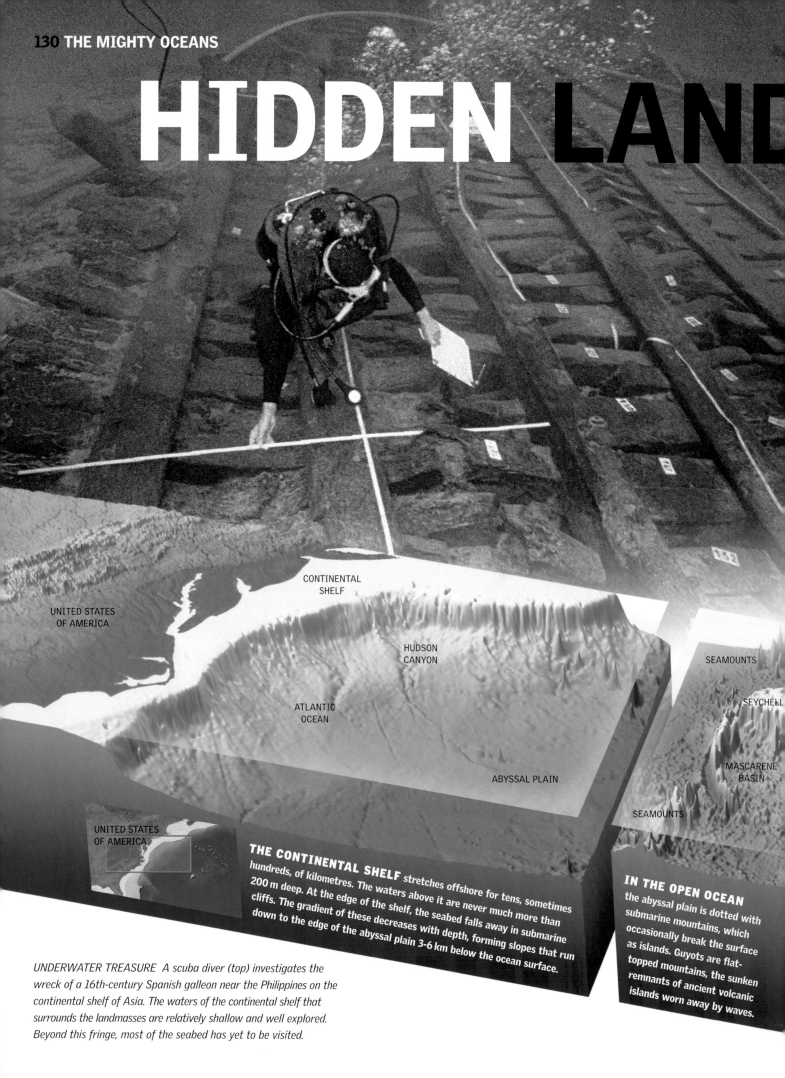

HIDDEN LAND

CONTINENTAL
SHELF

UNITED STATES
OF AMERICA

HUDSON
CANYON

SEAMOUNTS

SEYCHELL

ATLANTIC
OCEAN

MASCARENE
BASIN

ABYSSAL PLAIN

SEAMOUNTS

UNITED STATES
OF AMERICA

THE CONTINENTAL SHELF stretches offshore for tens, sometimes hundreds, of kilometres. The waters above it are never much more than 200 m deep. At the edge of the shelf, the seabed falls away in submarine cliffs. The gradient of these decreases with depth, forming slopes that run down to the edge of the abyssal plain 3-6 km below the ocean surface.

IN THE OPEN OCEAN the abyssal plain is dotted with submarine mountains, which occasionally break the surface as islands. Guyots are flat-topped mountains, the sunken remnants of ancient volcanic islands worn away by waves.

UNDERWATER TREASURE A scuba diver (top) investigates the wreck of a 16th-century Spanish galleon near the Philippines on the continental shelf of Asia. The waters of the continental shelf that surrounds the landmasses are relatively shallow and well explored. Beyond this fringe, most of the seabed has yet to be visited.

SCAPES

THE LARGEST TOPOGRAPHICAL FEATURE ON OUR PLANET LIES UNDER THE OCEANS. The so-called global mid-ocean ridge is a massive submarine mountain chain which circles the Earth, meandering from the north to the south of the Atlantic Ocean, around the bottom of Africa, across the Indian Ocean, then south of Australia and into the Pacific Ocean, where it winds its way northwards towards California. Its highest peaks rival those of the greatest mountain ranges on land and some break the surface to form islands. The best-studied section is the Mid-Atlantic Ridge, which rises an average of 4.5 km above the surrounding seafloor.

Deep-sea contours

The ocean floor is another world, but a world like ours with mountains, plains and canyons. Its geography lies hidden beneath huge masses of water and most of it lies in darkness. Understanding this world has been and is a slow process, and there is still much that we do not know. For most of history, the seabed has been little more than somewhere for ships' anchors to catch and settle. Only in recent decades has modern technology – including a new generation of submersibles and various forms of camera equipment – brought to light many deep-sea wonders. Nowadays, almost every dive into the deep ocean reveals a new inhabitant, another creature to add to the list of previously unknown species.

The first attempts to learn about the seafloor were made from ships, which lowered long lines until they hit the bottom. During the 19th century, these deep-line soundings became routine on research vessels in the Caribbean and Atlantic, and slowly they built up a rough picture of the seabed in these areas. In 1855, a bathymetric chart of the Atlantic was published, which first showed evidence of mountains in the centre of the ocean. With the development of echo-sounding systems during the First World War – primitive sonar, originally used to hunt down submarines – these charts became more detailed, confirming the existence of a chain of mountains in the Mid-Atlantic and showing the ocean floor to be much more rugged than had previously been thought.

Black smokers

Today, we know that mountain chain as the Mid-Atlantic Ridge. Like the rest of the global mid-ocean ridge, it was formed by volcanic activity, which not only gives rise to new crust but also creates extraordinary pockets of deep-sea life.

Seawater here seeps down through cracks in the Earth's crust, where the molten magma beneath heats it to temperatures of about 350°C. The superheated water then spouts out again through hydrothermal vents, like a series of submarine geysers, bringing with it a wealth of minerals and supporting unique life forms. These include giant tubeworms, which thrive here not by filter feeding like most of their relatives, but by obtaining the energy and nutrients they need from bacteria living in their own tissues. The bacteria in their turn survive by converting sulphur and other chemical compounds contained in the water pumped out from the vents. When these deep-sea geysers, or 'black smokers', were first discovered in 1977, they caused a sensation.

Since then, it has been speculated that life on Earth may have actually begun around such vents and even that similar vents on other planets or moons might support life of their own. The most likely candidate in the solar system has been flagged up as Europa, one of Jupiter's larger moons, known to have a surface of cracked water ice that is thought to cover deep liquid oceans.

The fact that we know so much about a satellite of a planet more than 600 million km away only underlines the extent of our ignorance of our own planet's deep-ocean floor. Vast regions of it are still unmapped and most of it has never been visited, either by manned or unmanned submarines. The black smokers may be only the first in a line of marvels waiting to be revealed.

JAPAN

INDIAN OCEAN

JAPAN

GUYOT

PACIFIC OCEAN

SOUTH HONSHU RIDGE

IZU-OGASAWARA TRENCH

SEYCHELLES

MADASCASGAR

HIDDEN BY THE SEA are massive mountain chains and canyons, or ridges and trenches. The deepest trenches occur not far from the continental shelf, near boundaries between tectonic plates, which also often give rise to volcanic ridges and islands. The largest underwater ridge is the global mid-ocean ridge, the world's greatest mountain range.

In 1990, for example, another self-supporting ecosystem was found at the bottom of the Gulf of Mexico, when submariners discovered a 'lake' of thick brine, whose shoreline was made up of densely concentrated beds of mussels. These mussels, a new species, contained bacteria that extracted energy from methane bubbling up from the seafloor. It was an oasis of life surrounded by a virtually barren abyssal plain and completely independent of energy from the Sun. Other unique animal species there included different kinds of worms, snails, crabs and shrimps.

Ocean chasms

Just as there are mountains and lakes on the seafloor, so there are valleys and canyons. The global mid-ocean ridge is bisected along its length by a deep, jagged rift, marking the boundary between two tectonic plates, which are here drawing apart from one another. In fact, the ridge can be thought of as two parallel mountain chains, one on each side of the diverging tectonic boundary, the result of new crust rising up from the Earth's interior. This rift is constantly evolving and changing its shape, albeit at a pace too slow to see. Every year, the Atlantic widens by a few centimetres (see pages 30-31).

The Pacific, meanwhile, is becoming smaller. Around its rim, tectonic plates are converging rather than diverging. Here, the crust of the oceanic plate is plunging beneath the thicker crust of the continents and their encircling shelves, and sinking slowly back into the Earth's interior. Where this happens deep-ocean trenches form. The deepest and most famous of these is the Mariana Trench, which lies around 2400 km east of the Philippines. From the surface to its deepest point, the Challenger Deep, is a drop of 10 920 m – Mount Everest could sit in it and still be covered by two kilometres of water.

When the US Navy bathyscape *Trieste* carried explorer and engineer Jacques Piccard and Navy lieutenant Don Walsh all the way to the bottom of the Mariana Trench, on January 23, 1960, they found it covered with a soft mud, made from the bodies of plankton that drift down from the water column above.

CRAMPED QUARTERS Most manned deep-sea submarines are small, with room for just one or two people. This picture was taken inside the submersible Alvin, *during an expedition to explore the Mid-Atlantic Ocean Ridge.*

Amazingly, they also saw living animals. They described these as 'shrimps', although samples were not taken and they have never been formally identified. Subsequent unmanned expeditions have found many simple life-forms in the Mariana Trench, including large numbers of foraminifera – primitive single-celled organisms that form shells.

The Mariana Trench is far from unique. The Philippine Trench, for example, is a 1320 km-long scar on the seabed, stretching north from Indonesia and along the eastern edge of the Philippines. Its deepest point, the Galathea Depth, lies 10 540 m under the ocean's surface. It is not only deep but wide, averaging around 30 km from one lip to the other. Not far from

VENT COMMUNITIES Minerals in the water pumped out by hydrothermal vents support their own ecosystems, whose inhabitants include giant tubeworms and eelpout fish, existing independent of light from the Sun.

its northern tip is the Ryukyu Trench (5212 m deep), heading north from Taiwan towards Japan, and from there a succession of trenches form a chain round the northern fringe of the Pacific as far as Alaska – the Japan, Kuril and Aleutian trenches.

Converging plates

These trenches form part of the Pacific's 'Ring of Fire'. Rather than sliding gently under the continental crust, the Pacific plate here moves in jolts. Huge frictional forces are built up and released as earthquakes. As the oceanic plate descends towards the mantle, it melts and sections bubble up to form magma chambers, which explode as volcanoes. Japan's Mount Fuji and many of the country's offshore islands were created in this way.

This process is not confined to the western Pacific. In the south Pacific, the Tonga Trench is part of another converging plate boundary. Its 9900 m chasm and the islands west of it have formed where the Pacific plate is being forced beneath the continental crust of Australasia. Convergence at

DEEP-SEA GEYSERS Submarine geysers in the mid-ocean ridges get their name 'black smokers' from the superheated water they pump out. It is laden with minute particles of iron, copper and zinc sulphides, which makes it look like thick clouds of underwater 'smoke'.

the Tonga Trench is taking place faster than anywhere else in the world: on average, 15 cm of the oceanic crust disappears here every year – in some years, as much as 24 cm is lost. On the opposite side of the Pacific is the longest trench in Earth's oceans, the 5900 km Peru-Chile Trench, skirting the western coastline of South America.

Similar deep-sea trenches, volcanoes and earthquake zones exist in the Indian and Atlantic Oceans and the Mediterranean Sea, but most of these trenches are shallower than those in the Pacific. This is not because the forces behind them are weaker, but because their bottoms have been filled up with sediment. Rifts in the oceanic crust near the mouths of large rivers, for instance, are often completely filled in with sand or mud.

SEAMOUNTS

IN ADDITION TO THE MID-OCEAN RIDGES, INDIVIDUAL MOUNTAINS CALLED SEAMOUNTS RISE DRAMATICALLY FROM THE OCEAN FLOOR. Towering thousands of metres above the surrounding abyssal plain, most are the remnants of volcanoes, the underwater equivalents of famous land mountains such as Kilimanjaro rising from the plains of Africa. Where they break the surface, they cease to be seamounts and become islands. Nevertheless, they can be considered as individual mountains, and by that definition the world's highest mountain is not land-based Everest, which peaks at 8850 m above sea level, but Hawaii's Mauna Kea, which rises to 10 203 m from seabed to summit.

In many ways, seamounts can be considered the underwater equivalent of islands, not just physically but from a biological point of view. Like islands, they often have their own endemic species, found nowhere else in the sea. They also act as 'stepping stones' for coastal-water creatures, helping them to spread to new areas. Fishermen are usually familiar with seamounts, as they tend to support large numbers of fish and other sea life. This is partly because of the upwelling that occurs around them as deep-water currents hit their slopes, and partly because of the range of habitats they provide at different heights. The upwelling brings nutrients from the seabed, which feed bacteria and algae, while the many outcrops, nooks and crannies provide anchor points and hiding places for a wide range of different types of animal.

Ocean hot spots

Seamounts form wherever volcanoes erupt from the ocean floor. They usually stand alone or as parts of archipelagos and are distinguished from the mountains in mid-ocean ridges by their circular or conical shapes. Most formed over hot spots, points where the oceanic crust sits over plumes of molten rock reaching up from the mantle. Hot spots are long-lived, producing chains of islands and seamounts as the tectonic plates of the Earth's crust move over them. The Azores, Galápagos and Hawaiian islands were all formed in this way, as were less well-known groups, such as the Foundation Chain in the south Pacific.

The most bountiful of all seamounts are those that have their peaks close to the surface. Here, the mixture of upwelling water and sunlight leads to an abundance of phytoplankton, the tiny photosynthesising organisms that form the basis of most marine food chains. The Bowie Seamount in the Gulf of Alaska off the coast of British Columbia, Canada, is a perfect example. Its peak is just 27 m below the surface, while its base is at 3150 m down in the depths. It supports clouds of juvenile rockfish and large shoals of black cod. Around its terraced peak, sculpted by waves during the Ice Age when sea levels were lower, are thickets of red algae and kelp. Among the fronds are giant scallops, sea anemones and starfish, as well as large predators such as the Pacific halibut and wolf eel.

GUYOTS

STRETCHED ACROSS THE PACIFIC, LIKE A LONG FINGER POINTING NORTH FROM THE WESTERNMOST TIP OF THE HAWAIIAN ARCHIPELAGO, is a chain of underwater mountains called the Emperor Seamount Chain. They were once volcanic islands, part of the Hawaiian archipelago, but over millions of years the tectonic plate underlying the Pacific inched its way north-westwards, and the islands gradually subsided below the ocean's surface. Now, almost all that is left of the former islands is a series of flat-topped submarine peaks, called guyots, lined up over some 3000 km of ocean.

While most seamounts are volcanoes that have never reached the surface, guyots – pronounced 'ghee-ohs', and named after the 19th-century Swiss-born Arnold Guyot, first professor of geology at Princeton University in the USA – are volcanic islands that have returned to the sea. Unlike other seamounts, they have relatively flat tops (hence their alternative name, tablemounts), the result of millions of years of wave erosion wearing their peaks down to nothing.

Many guyots are only just submerged, and in the tropics are crowned with coral reefs, forming atolls (see page 81). Bikini Atoll in the Marshall Islands, for example, sits on dead coral 1 km thick, built layer upon layer over millions of years on a guyot base. In some cases, the movement of tectonic plates has shifted guyots out of the tropics. Their table tops are capped with calcium carbonate, the remnants of a long-dead coral reef. Those moved from raised areas near the mid-ocean ridges now lie far beneath the waves. The tops of a few guyots are as much as 2 km below the sea's surface.

There are literally thousands of submarine volcanoes on the ocean floor, most extinct, and as with other seamounts, guyots exist in all the world's oceans. But they are most common in the western Pacific. For every one of the island groups scattered over the ocean surface in this region, dozens of seamounts and guyots dot its incredibly varied underwater landscape, while countless hills – mounds on the seabed less than 1000 m high – pepper the abyssal plain between them.

VOLCANIC CRESCENT The C-shaped rim of Molokini in Hawaii is all that remains above the sea's surface of a long extinct volcano. It demonstrates the way in which waves erode the tops of volcanic islands until, finally, they disappear beneath the sea to become guyots. Bottom: A submersible explores Molokini's steep sides. Both guyots and seamounts tend to have steeper slopes than mountains on land.

THE ICY SEAS

8

IN THE FAR NORTH AND SOUTH OF THE
PLANET, THE OCEANS ARE COVERED WITH
A THICK LAYER OF ICE. Despite the bleakness
of these ice caps, the waters beneath them are
filled with life. The Arctic and Southern oceans
contain some of the most productive waters
on Earth, and in spring and summer draw
migrating creatures from all over the globe.
Seabirds arrive in huge numbers to breed,
gorging themselves and feeding their young on
the abundant fish and other small animals to
be found in the water. Bigger migrants come
here, too, including baleen whales, the largest
creatures on Earth. Resident mammals are less
common, but include the Arctic harp seal (left).
Like other seals, it is protected from the cold
by an insulating layer of blubber. Other
creatures have their own unique ways of
coping with the icy water.

THE FROZEN FRONTIER

PUNCHING A WAY THROUGH If the deep sea is little known, the world under the ice is even more mysterious. Few craft have tried to map the seabed around the poles. Among those that have is the USS Hawksbill (below), a military submarine that began charting the floor of the Arctic Ocean in 1998.

THE POLAR SEAS ARE DIFFICULT AND DANGEROUS PLACES TO EXPLORE. In winter the entire Arctic basin is covered by ice that extends to the surrounding coasts of northern Canada and Eurasia, and the region is shrouded in darkness. Although the Sun returns in spring, and the ice cap melts around the edges and retreats, most of the Arctic Ocean remains covered and virtually inaccessible to humans. The Southern Ocean is also largely covered by ice during winter, and although it is accessible to ships at other times of the year, even then it is liable to sudden, violent storms that make diving expeditions deadly dangerous and scientific work from the surface all but impossible.

Neither of these inhospitable places were visited by humans until relatively recently. Inuit and other nomadic hunters frequented the fringes of the Arctic ice, but the ocean beneath was not even known to exist until the late 19th century. Antarctic waters also remained largely unexplored until the 19th century, when the first sealers and whaling ships arrived in the Southern Ocean.

Early polar journeys

The exploration of the Arctic region began with the first attempts to find a viable commercial sea route from Europe to Asia around the top of North America. The 15th-century navigator John Cabot (Giovanni Caboto) proposed the idea of a Northwest Passage in the 1490s. Over the next four centuries, numerous expeditions tried and failed to find a way through the maze of islands and broken sea ice off the northern coast of Canada, including the doomed expeditions of Henry Hudson in 1610 and Sir John Franklin in the 1840s. Finally, in 1906, the Norwegian explorer Roald Amundsen found a way through. The journey took three years and ultimately proved futile because the dynamic nature of the Arctic Ocean, with its ever-shifting icebergs and pack ice, meant that the passage constantly changed position and was frequently blocked, making it useless to commercial shipping.

Equally determined attempts were made to find a Northeast Passage round the top of northern Europe and Asia, culminating in the expedition made by Norwegian zoologist and explorer, Fridtjof Nansen, in 1893-6. Nansen's plan was to allow his ship, the *Fram*, to be frozen into the pack ice, then to drift through the ice across the North Pole. The *Fram* drifted for three years before it broke free. Nansen had expected to find shallow water in the Arctic basin, but soundings showed that the depth range was 3350-3960 m, establishing for the first time that a deep ocean basin existed there.

Scientific exploration

Towards the end of 1911, Roald Amundsen led another famous polar expedition, this time at the other end of the Earth. On December 14, he and his four companions became the first men ever to stand at the South Pole. Amundsen's expedition was the culmination of over two centuries of exploration there. In 1700, the English scientist Edmond Halley travelled aboard the first ship known to cross the Antarctic Convergence and enter what is now called the Southern Ocean. His ship, the *Pink Paramour*, was forced to turn back when it encountered gigantic icebergs, which Halley was the first person to sketch and describe.

On an expedition in the *Resolution* in 1772-5, James Cook became the first navigator known to cross the Antarctic Circle, but the ships that ventured into the Southern Ocean were mainly those of sealers. Their crews discovered many islands and probably included the first people to set foot on Antarctica itself. Most sealers kept quiet about what they found, however, as new islands meant new seal colonies to be exploited and profits depended on keeping them secret.

The scientific exploration of Antarctica and its waters did not properly begin until 1821 with the arrival of the Russian ship *Vostok* in the South Shetland Islands, off the Antarctic peninsula. The *Vostok*'s captain, Fabian Gottlieb von Bellingshausen, found the islands busy with sealers, counting no fewer than eight English and American ships.

The *Vostok* was the first of many expedition ships to reach the Southern Ocean, and research into the array of life forms under the Antarctic ice continues, while the ice itself provides a wealth of information about the planet. The Arctic Ocean is permanently covered by a floating ice cap, so most discoveries there have been made using submersibles or by divers venturing under the ice. New species are constantly being found. An expedition off Alaska in 2005 turned up 12 previously unknown species of animals, including jellyfish, sea cucumbers and brittle worms.

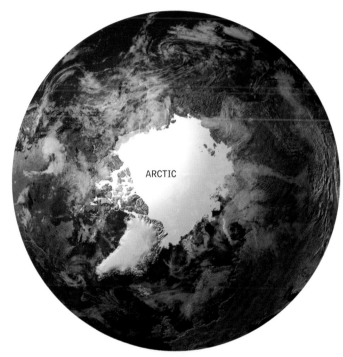

ARCTIC

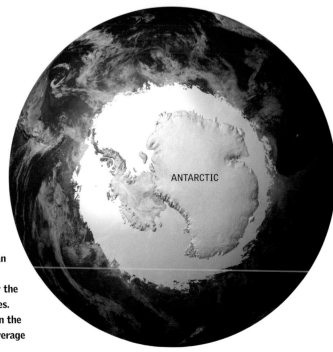

ANTARCTIC

WINTER ICE The ice caps of the Arctic and Antarctic shrink in summer and expand again as winter sets in. When sea ice covers the Arctic Ocean to its greatest extent, it is at a minimum around Antarctica, and vice versa. These illustrations show the farthest reach of winter ice around each of the poles. September 2005 saw the lowest extent of sea ice in the Arctic yet recorded, some 20 per cent below the average for 1988-2000.

ICEBERGS

STUNNING IN THEIR BEAUTY AND NOTORIOUS IN REPUTATION, ICEBERGS ARE ENDURING FEATURES OF THE NORTH ATLANTIC AND SOUTHERN OCEANS. These massive chunks of frozen fresh water break off from the leading edges of ice sheets and glaciers where they meet the sea – a process known as calving. To qualify as icebergs, they must stand at least 5 m proud of the water. Some are the size of a house; others are much bigger, measuring up to hundreds of kilometres across. Smaller chunks are known as bergy bits or, if they are too small to be a danger to shipping, as growlers.

The majority of icebergs in the Northern Hemisphere come from about 100 glaciers on the west coast of Greenland. These glaciers are among the fastest moving in the world. Forced along by the ever-expanding mass of ice and snow at the centre of the ice cap, they move at a rate of around 600 m a month. Every year they calve, on average, around 40 000 icebergs, which break off in a gradual but constant stream and clutter the far north of the Atlantic Ocean. Glacial icebergs are tall; many have great towers and peaks sculpted by the wind, earning them the name pinnacle or castle bergs.

Most icebergs in the Southern Ocean are calved from the floating ice shelf that extends out from the coast of Antarctica. They are flat-topped, or tabular, and the majority are much larger than glacial icebergs, breaking away to form floating islands that may persist for several decades.

Floating giants

Once calved, icebergs slowly but surely begin to melt and change shape, losing the sharp, angled edges of newly formed bergs and becoming gradually more curvaceous. Glacial bergs shrink slowly, eventually fading away to nothing. Tabular icebergs often break up, calving their own smaller icebergs. A few of these new icebergs roll over, exposing irregular, pitted undersides.

The tabular icebergs of the Southern Ocean can be truly enormous. Any that measure more than 16 km along at least one axis are given a name composed of a letter designating its place of origin and a number. In May 2000, a section of Antarctica's Ronne Ice Shelf broke away to form three massive tabular icebergs. The largest, designated A-43A, measured 172 km long and 33 km wide. The other two – A-43B and A-44 – were 85 km by 37 km and 66 km by 32 km respectively. These islands of ice have subsequently shrunk, but they are still floating in the Southern Ocean and are expected to last for several more decades.

Although dwarfed by the giant icebergs of the Southern Ocean, the castle bergs of the Arctic can themselves be huge. The largest reliably recorded towered 170 m above the sea surface.

Of course, most of an iceberg is hidden beneath the water, hence the phrase 'tip of the iceberg'. The amount that is concealed, which varies from around three to nine times the volume visible above the surface, depends on the salinity of the water in which it is floating. The less saline the water, the less buoyant it is and the lower an iceberg floats in it. An iceberg that is bulky enough to break through the hull of most vessels may have a relatively small tip showing at the surface, and even this can be virtually hidden in stormy seas.

Ancient ice

The ice from which icebergs form is very old. Those calved from the Greenland glaciers can contain snowflakes that fell 15 000 years ago. The tabular icebergs that break away from the Antarctic ice shelf can be even older. New ice constantly forms at accumulation points on the Antarctic ice sheet as snow falls and freezes, expanding and pushing away existing ice, which moves ever so slowly across the continent. In places the ice extends out over the sea, creating the floating ice shelves hundreds of metres thick from which tabular icebergs form. Scientists have estimated that a snowflake falling at the South Pole would take 50 000 years to reach the edge of the ice shelf. All the large tabular icebergs calved there contain ice that old.

Most icebergs are white, like the snow-covered ice sheets and glaciers from which they are born, but some are pale blue and a few even green. The whiteness of most bergs is the

ICEBERG PATROL The sinking of the SS *Titanic* by an iceberg in 1912 led to the formation of the International Ice Patrol (IIP), which monitors the shipping lanes between Europe and North America. The IIP's main area of operation is around the Grand Banks off Newfoundland, Canada, which the Labrador Current peppers with icebergs in spring and summer. Reconnaissance missions are carried out every few days using Hercules spotter planes, and the positions of all visible icebergs are fed into a computer along with data on the ocean currents and wind. The IIP then informs shipping of the location and predicted drift of any icebergs in the area.

MOON RISE OVER ANTARCTICA *The Sun gives the ice wall a golden glow as summer ends and winter starts to draw in. The Southern Ocean which surrounds Antarctica has the largest icebergs on Earth, formed from great chunks broken off from the ice shelf.*

result of light reflected by the snow and ice crystals within them. Blue icebergs consist of ice formed near the bottom of ice sheets and glaciers, where all the air and crystalline structure have been compressed out of it. This ice appears blue because it absorbs all other wavelengths of light, in the same way that deep water does. Green icebergs get their colour from microscopic algae, which grow on and within the undersides of most icebergs in spring and summer, and are exposed when an iceberg rolls over.

On the move

Icebergs are most commonly calved in the spring and summer months, when rising temperatures cause melting around the fissures from which they finally break off. The point of contact with the floating ice shelf or protruding glacier is further weakened before separation by the twice-daily vertical movement caused by the tides. Once an iceberg has been calved, surface currents push it along. Currents have a tendency to gather icebergs together. They appear in relatively large numbers, for example, off Newfoundland, gathered there by the Labrador Current, which picks them up off the west coast of Greenland and carries them down the eastern coast of Canada, like felled tree trunks in a river. From Newfoundland, the larger icebergs continue southwards at a speed of about 0.7 km/h, slowly melting as they go. A few reach as far south as Bermuda before finally disappearing, their journey from Greenland having taken as much as two years.

Icebergs are mainly moved by ocean currents. They are also affected by the wind to some extent, but smaller icebergs with large, flat surfaces above the water are more likely to be moved by the wind than big icebergs. Once set in motion, icebergs have massive momentum because of their huge bulk and they may drift for a long time.

Although most of Greenland's icebergs come from its western side, around 10 per cent are calved from glaciers on its eastern side, and very occasionally some of these travel southwards towards the north coast of Scotland. There have even been instances of icebergs travelling past Ireland, with the most southerly example in the eastern Atlantic being spotted around 320 km south of the Azores. Icebergs are rare in the northern North Pacific, but they are not unknown even there. They calve from the few glaciers that flow down to the Bering Sea from Alaska and Siberia. Occasionally, some work their way down from the Arctic Ocean itself through the Bering Strait and into the North Pacific.

Scientists have estimated that a snowflake falling at the South Pole would take 50 000 years to reach the edge of the Antarctic ice cap. All the large tabular icebergs calved there contain ice that old.

ALL ABOARD Icebergs provide floating platforms where penguins can rest. Some icebergs may last for months or even years before finally melting away to nothing, diluting the cold salty brine of the ocean with their fresh water.

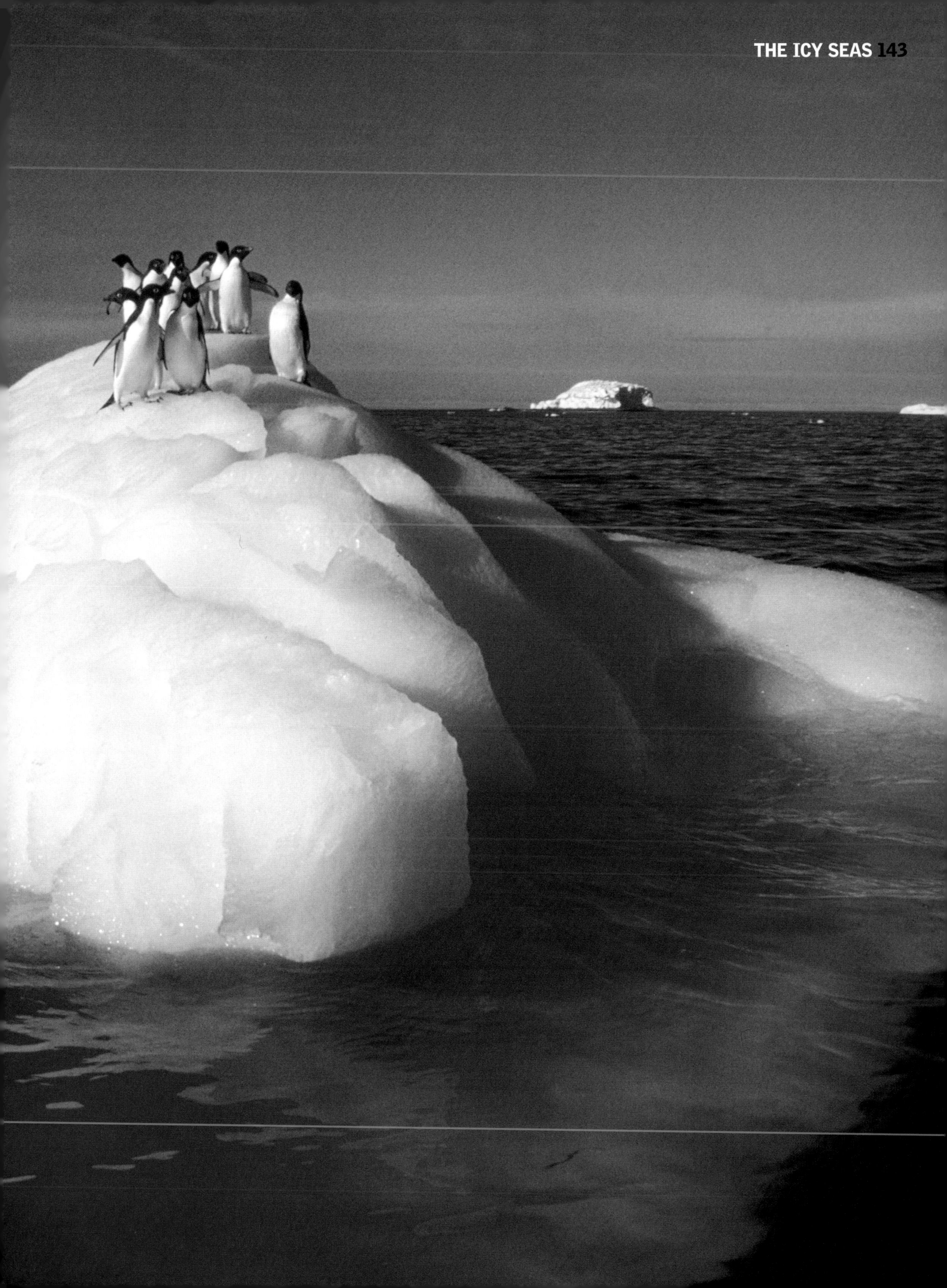

SEA ICE

UNLIKE THE ICEBERGS IT SOMETIMES ENTRAPS, SEA ICE CONTAINS SOME SALT. It forms on the surface of the oceans, extending out from the edges of the permanent ice caps every winter and retreating back as summer returns. It covers, on average, about 7 per cent of the world's oceans. Although it may break up and scatter in summer, it never completely disappears.

This quantity of ice has a major effect on the global climate. Not only does it form a solid layer between the ocean and the air, reducing the moisture and heat transfer between them, but it also reflects a huge amount of solar radiation back into space. Despite the abundance of sea ice around the poles, its existence is precarious. Nowhere is it more than 4 m thick, and current evidence shows that it is gradually disappearing, from the Arctic at least, as a result of global warming. Based on the rate of retreat observed so far, computer models predict that the Arctic Ocean will be completely free of ice in summer by 2080. If this happens, the Earth will absorb more sunlight than before, accelerating the warming process, and more moisture will be absorbed by the atmosphere, altering weather patterns. The disappearance of Arctic ice in summer will also change the ecology of the region. Many species, such as the polar bear, are specially adapted to living and feeding on the ice. They will almost certainly be unable to cope with the change and may face extinction.

Frazil, nilas and pancakes

Sea ice forms in clearly defined stages, the first of which is the creation of frazil, or grease ice. Grease ice begins to form when the air temperature at the ocean surface drops consistently below -1.8°C (because of its salt content, seawater has a lower freezing point than fresh water). Tiny disc-shaped ice crystals start to appear in the surface water. Gradually, these grow into hexagonal crystals with arms, like snowflakes. The slightest turbulence, even ripples created by a light breeze, cause these fragile shapes to break up, leaving a mass of ice fragments in the water. They gradually accumulate to form a suspension of increasing density, a mobile slush that is grease ice proper.

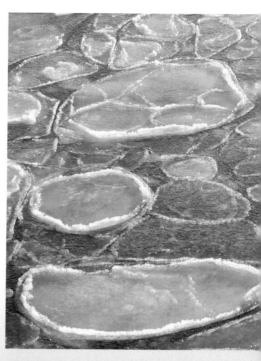

PANCAKE ICE This appears around the ice caps. It gets its name from the rounded shapes it forms, with each 'pancake' having a raised lip. As winter progresses, pancake ice slowly freezes together to form a solid sheet.

WALRUSES ON ARCTIC ICE Sea ice forms from ocean water and contains salt. The expansion of the ice caps in winter is due to the creation of new sea ice, which floats as a thin crust on the sea.

In calm conditions, the individual crystals within grease ice soon freeze together to form a thin, continuous sheet of ice, known as nilas. As the ice grows thicker, it changes colour. When it is just a few centimetres thick, it begins to lose transparency and is known as dark nilas. As it grows thicker, it gradually becomes lighter grey and less translucent, until it is opaque. At this point it is reflecting virtually all light and looks white.

Once the slushy frazil has frozen together as nilas, a new growth process starts. Water molecules begin to freeze to the bottom of the ice sheet, extending it downwards. This process leads to the creation of first-year ice. In a single season, this can reach 1.5-2 m thick.

Nilas forms only under relatively calm conditions. Out in the open ocean, where seas are rough, the waves prevent a solid ice sheet forming. Here, the grease ice builds up in an ever-denser suspension. Wave action periodically compresses areas of this grease ice, which freezes together as small cakes of slush. These grow larger as more grease ice freezes to their edges and more solid as the crystals within them freeze more tightly together. They slowly extend outwards to form rough ovals and circles, and as they collide with each other, pushed around by wave action, they develop raised rims. They are just a few centimetres thick around the edge, but deepen towards the centre. The largest can be up to 5 m in diameter and 70 cm thick. Collectively, these cakes of compressed slush are known as pancake ice.

With the onset of winter, pancake ice extends outwards from the poles, gradually calming any surface wave action. Eventually, some distance behind the ice's leading edge, the water is quiet enough for individual pancakes to freeze together, forming larger floes that gradually join up into a continuous sheet of first-year ice, known as consolidated pancake ice.

Unlike the flat first-year ice that forms from nilas, consolidated pancake ice tends to be bumpy and jagged. Pancakes collide and push together, tipping each other onto their sides or riding on top of one another before freezing together, with frazil acting as 'glue' between them. As a result of all this upheaval, the ice sheet is much thicker in some places than others, and its underside is very uneven. This rough bottom provides a perfect surface for algae to grow on, and numerous hiding places for krill and small fish. Most of the ice is thin enough to allow plenty of light to penetrate, resulting in an extremely productive ecosystem.

Multi-year ice

Although seawater loses some of its salt as it freezes, first-year ice is nonetheless still quite salty. As ice ages to become multi-year ice, it gradually becomes less saline, a process driven primarily by the summer melt. During winter, all sea ice is covered with snow. As summer advances, this snow begins to thaw, forming pools of fresh water on the surface of the ice. These pools absorb more of the Sun's energy than does the ice surrounding them and gradually warm up, melting the ice beneath. Eventually, the melting process may penetrate right

through the ice, forming thaw holes. The fresh meltwater that resulted from the thawed snow drains through the holes. Being less dense than seawater, this water remains at the sea surface beneath the ice, freezing to its underside as temperatures begin to drop again when summer ends.

The formation of thaw holes reduces the overall salinity of multi-year sea ice, but much more effective is the process by which meltwater gradually works down into the ice through tiny pores, channels and veins. This process, known as flushing, eventually drives out most of the remaining salt, resulting in ice that is not only made virtually entirely of fresh water, but is also much stronger than first-year ice, as its crystalline structure is uninterrupted by salt molecules.

Around half of all sea ice in the Arctic is multi-year ice. Some of it is transported around the Arctic Ocean by the Beaufort Gyre (see page 37), a journey that takes between seven and ten years. The remainder is drawn across and out of the Arctic basin by the East Greenland Current. The ice enters the Greenland Sea, where it cools the surface so much that new grease and pancake ice forms there in winter. The salt that is expelled during this ice formation enters the surface

ICED-IN Vladivostok, Russia's chief port on the Pacific, experiences an average winter temperature of -13°C, enough to cause the sea round about to freeze over. For several months of the year icebreakers are needed to keep the port open to commercial and military shipping.

water, increasing its density. This causes the surface water to sink to the seabed, forming part of the driving force behind the ocean conveyor belt (see page 38).

At home on the ice

Sea ice is an integral part of the Arctic and Southern Ocean ecosystems. It provides a structure on and within which bacteria and other microorganisms, such as algae, can live and grow. These in turn support a complex food web that includes everything from tiny zooplankton and krill to the largest predators. Most polar animals are directly or indirectly dependent on sea ice for food.

A few creatures even live on the ice. In the Arctic, it is the main haunt of the polar bear, which roams its white wastes in search of seals. Wandering bears are often shadowed by another, smaller mammal, the Arctic fox. Like foxes the world over it is an opportunist, feeding on a wide range of small prey. Out on the ice, it relies on the polar bear to do the hunting, surviving on discarded scraps. Like the polar bear, the Arctic fox is highly adapted for life in freezing conditions. Its extremities, such as its ears, are small to minimise heat loss, while its paws are densely furred to keep them warm and to give a grip on the snow. From early autumn to late spring, the fox's fur is pure white for camouflage and extremely thick to keep out the cold. When the sea ice retreats, it follows the polar bear back onto land, and sheds its dense winter coat for a more lightweight one coloured brown and grey.

As well as being a seasonal home to a small number of land mammals, sea ice provides air-breathing marine creatures with places to haul out and rest. Walruses, seals and penguins all use ice floes in this way, sometimes gathering on them in large numbers. One penguin species – the emperor – actually mates, lays its eggs and raises its chicks on the ice. The emperor is the largest of the penguin species, and the only one to spend the winter out on the Antarctic ice. Its breeding cycle takes longer than those of most other birds, so rather than laying its eggs in spring for them to hatch in midsummer, like the majority of Antarctic penguins, it gathers in large colonies on the sea ice in autumn – March to early April. Birds pair and mate, then in May or June the female lays a single large egg and passes it to the male. Shortly afterwards the females return to the sea to feed, leaving the males to incubate the eggs.

Emperor penguin eggs take around 65 to 70 days to hatch, during which time the males remain on the sea ice without feeding, huddling together for warmth through the long Antarctic night. As spring approaches and the Sun creeps above the horizon for a short time each day, the eggs hatch. The females return around the end of the incubation period to look after the hatchlings so the males can return to the sea for a time. A male can feed his chick for about 10 days on fluid brought up from his stomach if his partner does not return in time. The parents alternate feeding trips with looking after the hatchling through summer, as the open sea gets closer. In December or January, the chicks leave the breeding site for the sea.

VITAL STATISTICS

LATIN NAME: *Ursus arctos*
AVERAGE WEIGHT: Male 350-650 kg; female 150-250 kg
MAXIMUM RECORDED WEIGHT: 1002 kg
HABITAT: Land and sea ice within and near the
 Arctic Circle
CUBS: Between one and four, born between November
 and January
MAXIMUM RECORDED AGE: 32 years in the wild;
 41 years in captivity

THE WORLD'S LARGEST LAND PREDATOR,

AN ADULT MALE POLAR BEAR CAN WEIGH AS MUCH AS 10 MEN, AND REARED UP ON ITS BACK LEGS CAN REACH 3.4 M TALL. Polar bears are perfectly adapted to life in the Arctic, with dense, luxuriant fur and a thick layer of fat beneath the skin to keep out the cold. Their enormous paws spread their weight as they walk over sea ice, making it less likely to break beneath them, while in water their paws make very effective paddles, enabling them to swim easily between ice floes in the endless search for food.

Because of their icy habitat, polar bears are the most carnivorous of all bears, feeding almost exclusively on meat. They hunt mainly ringed and bearded seals. Seals are mammals and must come to the surface to breathe. Polar bears wait on the ice near breathing holes and grab the seals by the head as they come up for air. They also stalk seals that have hauled out onto the ice, approaching stealthily from downwind before charging in for the kill. Polar bears also scavenge on the carcasses of larger animals, including whales. In summer, when the sea ice retreats, they can become stranded on land and have to make do with smaller prey, such as seabirds and rodents. Like other bears they also eat eggs, berries or vegetation, when meat is not available.

Polar bears wander long distances in search of food. They have an excellent sense of smell, which leads them to carcasses and living prey, including seal cubs concealed beneath the ice. Because food can be scarce they sometimes go for days without eating, and when they make a kill or find carrion they gorge themselves, consuming up to a fifth of their own bodyweight. Their digestive systems are highly efficient at converting this food into the fat that provides them with warmth and energy, with 97 per cent of what they eat being assimilated into the body.

POLAR
BEAR

**NATURE'S
POWERS**

BREAKING THE ICE

BEFORE THE ADVENT OF PURPOSE-BUILT ICEBREAKERS AT THE BEGINNING OF
THE 20TH CENTURY, ICE-STRENGTHENED SHIPS WERE USED FOR VENTURING INTO
POLAR SEAS. Wooden sailing ships of conventional design had extra planking added
to the hull, particularly around the waterline, and cross-members were fixed inside,
in the hope that it would withstand the pressure imposed by the ice if the ship
became trapped between expanding floes. Later designs incorporated bands of
iron strapped around the outside of the ship, which was sometimes reinforced with
additional sheets of metal attached to the bow, stern and keel. These were designed
to help a ship push through the ice as well as to protect it from being crushed.
Despite these modifications, wooden ships were extremely vulnerable in heavy ice.
Early polar expeditions saw many ships sunk, while others became trapped in the
ice and were slowly crushed.

     One 19th-century ship proved indomitable in polar
conditions. The *Fram* was purpose-built for polar exploration
and became the most famous ship of its day. Captained by
Fridtjof Nansen, it survived the winter of 1893-4 trapped
in the Arctic ice. Unlike other ships of the time, it had been
designed with a rounded hull so that as the ice froze around it,
the ship was lifted up out of danger rather than being caught
between expanding floes.

     In contrast, the *Endurance*, which carried Sir Ernest
Shackleton and his expedition team to the Antarctic in the
winter of 1914, had originally been designed for tourist cruises
in the Arctic, and did not have a rounded hull. As the ice took
hold and squeezed, the ship did not rise out of harm's way.
The *Endurance* remained entombed until the following spring,
by which time its hull had been crushed. When the ice around
the ship melted, it promptly sank.

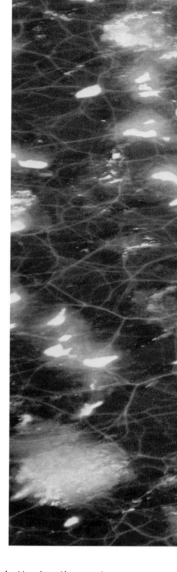

*DRIVING FORCE An
icebreaker smashes a path
through the ice in Thunder
Bay, Ontario, Canada.
Icebreakers keep the shipping
lanes open and are vital to
the trade of many towns
and cities in and around
the Arctic.*

Crash and smash

Modern purpose-built ice-breaking ships are among the most
powerful ships for their size. They are made from a type of steel
that has optimum strength at low temperatures in order to
withstand crashing into the edge of the ice. The hull is unusually
thick at the bow, stern and waterline, and flat-bottomed. There
is no keel, or other protruding stabilisers, that the ice could get
a grip on. The bows slope, like the upturned ends of skis, and
the ships are built to be unusually heavy.

     To create a passage, an icebreaker approaches the ice at
full speed. On contact, the ship's sloping bows ride up onto the
ice, so that the weight of the ship bears down and smashes
through it. The rounded hull deflects the broken chunks of ice
away from the ship so it can keep moving forwards. An 'ice
horn' fitted over the rudder and propellers protects them when
the ship moves in reverse; an 'ice knife' at the stern brushes
aside broken fragments to keep them away from these moving
parts when the ship is travelling forwards. Other modifications
include high-pressure air jets, which force bubbles under the ice
before the ship hits it. This layer of air exerts extra pressure on
the ice from below, making it easier to break. Heated water jets
are also used below the waterline to make the ice more fragile.

While these modifications help to shatter ice, the most
important feature of an icebreaker is its engine. These ships
have enormously powerful engines for their size. Some have
massive diesel engines with extra force supplied by gas
turbines; others are nuclear-powered to provide the necessary
amount of thrust to drive the ship up on top of the ice.

     The biggest ice-strengthened ship ever to sail was a
monster called the *Manhattan*. Created from a converted oil
tanker, it was relaunched in its new form on August 24, 1969.
The *Manhattan* was built to transport oil from a newly
discovered source in Prudhoe Bay on the north coast of Alaska.
After successfully completing its maiden voyage, accompanied
by the Canadian icebreaker, *John A. Macdonald*, it returned
with a symbolic cargo of one barrel of oil. Although the
Manhattan had proved that the journey to the icebound oil field
was possible for a ship of its size, the voyage was never
repeated. The cost of the journey and the time it took made it
economically unviable. Environmental concerns were also raised,
and it was decided to build a pipeline from the oilfield to Valdez
on Prince William Sound, on Alaska's south-eastern coast.

UP AND AWAY A researcher launches a weather balloon from an icebreaker high in the Arctic. The halo around the Sun in this picture is not a trick of photography but a natural phenomenon, caused by ice crystals in the atmosphere.

LEADS & POLYNYA

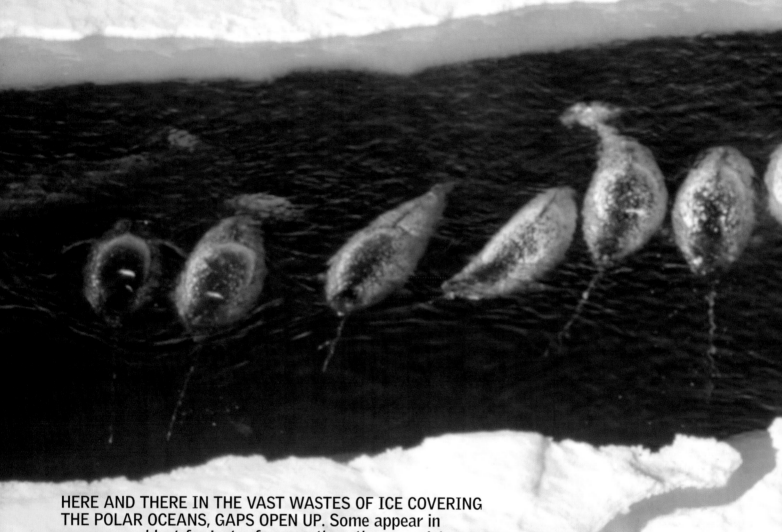

HERE AND THERE IN THE VAST WASTES OF ICE COVERING THE POLAR OCEANS, GAPS OPEN UP. Some appear in summer and last for just a few months; others persist even through the winter. Either way, they are vital to the survival of marine mammals, and they give land-dwellers and birds a chance to catch food in the rich polar waters. Because these gaps in the ice are associated with upwelling waters that bring up nutrients from the ocean floor, especially in the Antarctic, they are among the most productive areas of water in the world's oceans.

Leads – temporary lifelines

During spring and summer, wave action can cause ice floes to sheer past one another, or even to part company. The resulting cracks, known as leads, vary from a few metres to several kilometres wide. As temperatures rise and leads extend, some split into branches and others link up, creating networks of channels along which marine mammals such as seals and whales can travel. Leads also open up the polar waters to birds, which use them to reach food under the ice. In the Arctic, polar bears wait near leads for seals to surface, or travel alongside them in search of prey. Leads also aid ships, even in winter, as the ice that forms between them is generally thinner than elsewhere and can be smashed more easily by icebreakers and surfacing submarines.

TUSK FORCE Leads act as natural highways through sea ice for whales and other marine mammals. In the Arctic Ocean, narwhals use them to reach new hunting grounds and as places to rest between foraging trips far below the surface.

Leads also have an impact on the weather. Where they form, relatively warm ocean water is exposed to the colder atmosphere, allowing heat and moisture to gather in the air above. Low-level clouds often bubble up just downwind of leads and water vapour can be seen rising off them. As autumn sets in and leads begin to freeze over, they deposit salt into the sea. This denser water tends to sink and is replaced by displaced water forced up from below, promoting the mixing and upwelling of nutrients from the seabed.

Polynyas – open water

While leads are seasonal and often short-lived, polynyas are more permanent and frequently persist through the winter. They, too, are areas of open water surrounded by ice, but unlike leads they tend to be roughly circular or oval in shape. They occur where warmer water wells up from the deep, and near land coastlines where prevailing winds blow newly formed ice out to sea. In winter, polynyas may be the only places where marine mammals can reach air. Seals, whales and walruses congregate in them, waiting out the dark winter months until the spring thaw arrives. Being more permanent than leads, polynyas cause more persistent upwelling and so are even richer than leads in nutrients. Phytoplankton thrives in them, and the fish that feed on it attract fish-eating birds.

CLEAR WATER Polynyas often form along coastlines, such as here in the Bering Sea, off the coast of St Lawrence Island (solid green area). In this false-colour satellite image, the red area is newly created frazil, which constantly forms on the surface of the polynya and is blown away from the coastline towards the older, more solid sea ice (broken yellow/green areas).

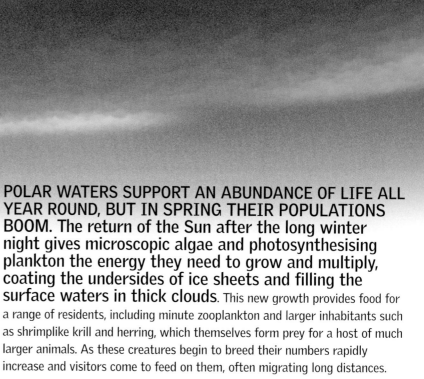

LIFE UNDER ICE

POLAR WATERS SUPPORT AN ABUNDANCE OF LIFE ALL YEAR ROUND, BUT IN SPRING THEIR POPULATIONS BOOM. The return of the Sun after the long winter night gives microscopic algae and photosynthesising plankton the energy they need to grow and multiply, coating the undersides of ice sheets and filling the surface waters in thick clouds. This new growth provides food for a range of residents, including minute zooplankton and larger inhabitants such as shrimplike krill and herring, which themselves form prey for a host of much larger animals. As these creatures begin to breed their numbers rapidly increase and visitors come to feed on them, often migrating long distances.

Air-breathers

Summer visitors to polar waters include several species of baleen whale, such as the blue, humpback and grey whales. Only one baleen species, the bowhead, is a permanent Arctic resident – its largest. The bowhead is the only baleen whale to give birth in polar waters, calving between March and August, when food is at its most plentiful.

The bowhead is very well adapted to life in the Arctic Ocean, where it lives around the margins of the sea ice in summer and under the advancing ice in winter. Its massive head – which makes up almost one-third of its

overall length – doubles as an icebreaker, capable of creating breathing holes in ice as much as 30 cm thick. The bowhead's 70 cm thick layer of blubber serves as a bodywarmer, protecting its internal organs from the cold, and also provides a food reserve during the long winter. It has the longest baleen strainers of any whale, with which it sifts plankton just 2.5 cm long from the icy waters. Even at birth, the bowhead is designed for life at low temperatures. Newborn calves are more barrel-shaped than those of other whale species, an adaptation that lowers their surface-area-to-mass ratio and so minimises the amount of skin through which they can lose heat.

Several species of the smaller toothed whales inhabit polar waters. Narwhals and belugas, like the bowhead, are Arctic residents. Both are social species, living in small, close-knit groups that sometimes gather together, forming herds that may contain hundreds or even thousands of animals. The narwhal is a diver that finds much of its food at the bottom, while the beluga, or white whale, forages for food such as fish and crustaceans on the undersides of the ice as well as on the ocean floor. Neither species has a dorsal fin, so they can swim just under the ice in search of breathing holes.

The beluga is thought to have the most sophisticated sonar apparatus of any whale, allowing it to hunt and navigate even in dark waters under thick ice. The sonar, which it can use to receive surface-reflected echoes, may also help it to locate breathing holes. In winter, belugas can become trapped beneath the ice and only survive by keeping these holes open through constant activity. Some fall victim to polar bears, which dive into the breathing holes to catch them.

Another predator of both belugas and narwhals, and even the bowhead, is the killer whale, which frequents both Arctic and Antarctic waters. Killer whales do not usually go under the ice, but patrol its edges in search of seals, penguins and fish as well as other whale species. They also seek out seals and penguins on the ice itself, lifting their heads above the waves in a behaviour known as 'spyhopping'. Some groups have developed special techniques for dislodging prey from floating ice floes (see pages 100-101).

Polar seals spend more time than whales under the ice, although they haul out to rest and to give birth to their young. Like all mammals they have to breathe air, and they create holes in the ice to which they return regularly. The Weddell seal of the Antarctic, which lives in areas of permanent ice cover, maintains its breathing holes by rasping the ice with its teeth.

While under the ice seals are out of the reach of killer whales, and as fish that live under the ice have no other air-breathing predators, this puts seals near the top of a food chain that is beyond the range of narwhals and belugas. They thrive in polar waters and are more common there than anywhere else. The crabeater seal, which lives under the Antarctic ice and feeds on krill, is one of the most numerous marine mammals on Earth, with a global population of around 13 million.

Some seals inhabit the waters between ice cap and land. In the Antarctic, the leopard seal hugs the fringes of the sea ice, where it hunts for penguins, while walruses live either among the broken Arctic sea ice or out in open water. Unlike most seals, which are active hunters, walruses seek easier prey. They search for shellfish on the sea bottom, which they find using their tusks and long, sensitive whiskers. Walruses also squirt water with their mouths to expose shellfish hidden in the sediment. They often clamber out onto ice floes to rest, but can sleep in the water, expanding air sacs in their throat, like natural water wings, to keep them afloat.

Avian aquatics

Walruses, like polar bears, are exclusive to the Arctic. Their counterparts in the Antarctic are the penguins. Penguins are found only in the Southern Hemisphere, and around half the penguin species live in waters surrounding Antarctica. Of all birds, they are the best adapted to life in the sea. Their wings, incapable of flight, have evolved into stiff and powerful paddles, while their bodies are smooth and torpedo-shaped to help them cut through the water. Like most seals, penguins are active hunters that feed on fish, squid and krill. Although all Antarctic penguins will eat any of these creatures if the opportunity presents itself, different species have adapted to hunting different prey.

The two largest species, the king and emperor penguins, mainly hunt squid and have long, pincer-like beaks to help them grasp their long-bodied, fast-moving prey. They feed in the open ocean and in polynyas (see pages 150-51). Both species make impressive dives to find food and often hunt at depths where their prey is virtually hidden in darkness. Emperor penguins often make dives to more than 400 m – the deepest recorded is 565 m. Smaller Antarctic penguins, such as the Adelie and chinstrap, eat krill and small fish, and have shorter, stubbier beaks. All penguins have backward-pointing spines on their tongues to help them hold on to their wet, slippery meals.

Fishy adaptations

Fish that live beneath the ice have their own adaptations to help them survive. Many, such as the various species of Antarctic ice fish, have special proteins in their blood that act as a natural antifreeze. These proteins ensure that the creatures' blood remains liquid at temperatures as low as -2.5°C, slightly lower than the temperature of -1.8°C at which the most salt-laden seawater freezes.

A surprising variety of fish live under the ice of both the Arctic and Southern oceans, but most species are relatively small. The largest in the Southern Ocean is the Patagonian toothfish, which ranges from 70–215 cm long. This relatively limited size is because polar fish have slow metabolisms, which produce correspondingly slow growth rates. Being cold-blooded, these creatures are unable to generate their own heat, so their body temperature remains about the same as that of the water around them, and this slows down the essential processes of life.

There is one exception to this rule – the Greenland or sleeper shark which inhabits the Arctic Ocean, including waters beneath the permanent ice. It is the world's second-largest predatory shark after the great white, reaching lengths of up to 6.5 m and weighing well over 2 tonnes. Like most polar fish the Greenland shark moves slowly most of the time in order to conserve energy, but when hunting it can put on great bursts of speed. In the southern part of its range it hunts fast-moving species such as salmon, but its diet is not confined to fish. Like most sharks, the Greenland is an opportunistic hunter and scavenger that feeds on a wide range of prey. One specimen that was caught and examined by scientists was found to have an entire reindeer in its stomach.

Spineless wonders

Huge numbers of invertebrates live in the polar seas, including squid and jellyfish, sea jellies, salps, molluscs, sponges and crustaceans. Although they are more numerous in open water, many live under the ice. Some polar invertebrate species are

COLD-BLOODED SURVIVORS Desmonema glaciale *is the largest Antarctic jellyfish; it preys on fish under the ice. Antarctic ice fish (opposite) have proteins in their blood that act as a natural antifreeze, keeping it liquid even at temperatures below 0°C.*

much larger than related species found in warmer regions. Among them are the ferocious colossal squid of the Southern Ocean (see pages 118-119) and the world's largest jellyfish, the Arctic lion's mane. This enormous drifting animal feeds on fish and other swimming creatures, which it catches in its stinging tentacles. These can reach over 30 m long and trail behind the jellyfish's body, a pulsing bell that can measure up to 2.5 m in diameter. In Antarctica, 2 m-high sponges have been found, whereas related species living off the coast of Vancouver, Canada, only grow to about 20 cm. The size of these creatures is explained by their lifespans. Although they are cold-blooded and hence slow-growing in frigid waters, the stable environment under the ice enables them to live for a long time.

Most invertebrates are prey for fish and other predators, and perhaps the most important prey creatures of all are the krill. Several species of these free-swimming crustaceans live

CRUSTACEAN FEAST *Krill underpin the Antarctic food chain, forming vast swarms in spring and summer that provide food for great numbers of seabirds, fish and other predators.*

throughout the world's oceans, including the Arctic, but they are most numerous in the waters around Antarctica. They feed on phytoplankton, which they filter out of the water, and on algae, which they scrape off the undersides of the ice. Adult krill reach about 6 cm in length.

Although krill are found in huge quantities in the open ocean, they form even denser swarms under the ice. Research in Antarctica has found a band of krill between 1 and 13 km from the edge of the ice that is five times more concentrated than krill in open water. One species in particular, *Euphausia superba*, forms gigantic swarms in the Antarctic, providing food in spring and summer for a multitude of other creatures, from fish and birds to seals and whales. Each swarm can contain millions of individuals. Scientists estimate that there are around 500 000 billion krill alive in the oceans at any one time, the equivalent of around 80 000 for every human being on Earth.

INDEX

PICTURE CREDITS

NATURE'S MIGHTY POWERS: THE MIGHTY OCEANS
was published by The Reader's Digest Association Ltd,
London. It was created and produced by Reader's Digest
with Toucan Books Ltd, London.

The Reader's Digest Association Ltd,
11 Westferry Circus,
Canary Wharf,
London E14 4HE
www.readersdigest.co.uk

First edition Copyright © 2006
Reprinted 2007

Written by
Daniel Gilpin

FOR TOUCAN BOOKS
Editors Helen Douglas-Cooper, Andrew Kerr-Jarrett
Picture researchers Wendy Brown, Mia Stewart-Wilson,
Christine Vincent, Caroline Wood
Proofreader Marion Dent
Indexer Michael Dent

FOR READER'S DIGEST
Project editor Christine Noble
Art editor Julie Bennett
Senior designer Austin Taylor
Pre-press account managers Penny Grose, Sandra Fuller
Product production manager Claudette Bramble
Production controller Katherine Bunn

READER'S DIGEST, GENERAL BOOKS
Editorial director Julian Browne
Art director Anne-Marie Bulat

Colour origination Colour Systems Ltd, London
Printed in China

We are committed to both the quality of our products and
the service we provide to our customers. We value your
comments, so please feel free to contact us on 08705 113366
or via our website at **www.readersdigest.co.uk**

If you have any comments or suggestions about the content of
our books, you can email us at **gbeditorial@readersdigest.co.uk**